Sₗᵢₘ ᵥᵢₜₕ Hᵢₘ

A guide to slimming using grace, faith and common sense.

By

Andrea Thornhill

For Joe

Slim with Him is a guide to slimming in an effortless way. It uses the grace that has freely been given to us by Christ, and encourages us to get closer to God, so that our needs will be met through Him, rather than food or a crash diet.

CONTENTS

INTRODUCTION

A friend once asked me, what my secret for staying slim was, and the answers I gave were surprising! As I realised, accidentally, I had followed biblical principles of faith, in regard to my weight and shape, all my life without knowing it.

I think these principles can help anyone and the faith it takes to be slim, can also be used in other areas as well, such as healing and prosperity. Some of these principles can be used even if you're not a Christian, as God's laws work for everyone, just like the law of gravity. However, I would say, with God's help and His Holy Spirit, it'll be a lot easier!

Although I look quite chubby in my baby photographs, I've always been slim. As a child, people would describe me as skinny and I would be called names like Beanpole and Lanky. Family used to force me to eat and my nan would feed me jam doughnuts. I used to hate being skinny and I used to hate being forced to eat (although I quite liked the doughnuts!).

I started ballet at four, and as a teenager went to full-time dancing school, where I boarded. There, everyone was body conscious. We danced in front of full-length

> We were obsessed with food and dieting.

mirrors every day, in nothing but leotards and tights, and we were weighed each week. We were all obsessed with food and dieting and this carried on when I became a professional dancer, for eight years after.

Now, as a middle-aged woman, wife and mother, I find it takes a bit more effort to stay in control of my weight, and need the principles outlined in this book more than ever. I don't believe it comes naturally (being in my genes) and I feel as though I could pile on the pounds as much as anyone, but I don't, as I live by these guidelines.

My intention in writing this book, is not to offend anyone and please forgive me if this happens, instead it's to inspire, encourage and provide different outlooks when approaching the area of weight loss. I have no diet to give you, just lots of tips and suggestions of ways you can change your life through lifestyle, rather than the number of calories being consumed.

I haven't had any formal training in nutrition or health and so the advice I give is from experience, a lot of study and meditation, and inspiration from the Holy Ghost. I have been a Christian all my life but really came to know Christ when I was eleven. I asked the Holy Spirit to live in me and we have never been parted since! When I went to boarding school, I lost my way for a few years, but Jesus never forsook me, waiting for me, until I was ready to devote my life to Him again. Once I did that, I never looked back again. He's everything to me, He guides me, protects me, loves me, wants me. He impacts me in everything I do, I love Him completely, trust Him wholeheartedly and listen to Him as much as possible. If you haven't got Jesus in your life already and want Him, just ask. Pray and ask Him to be Master of your life, thank Him for going to the cross and rising from the dead, and spend time getting to know Him through the bible, it's as simple as that.

Personally, I believe every Word of the bible right from the world being created in six days to the second coming that hasn't happened yet. (There is plenty of scientific proof available for

> The Word of God is so much more powerful than my words could ever be.

creation – if you need it. Just get yourself on the Internet and do some research! Creation.com is great.) Hence, I use a lot of scriptures throughout this book, please don't skim through them. The Word of God is so much more powerful than my words could ever be. It has the ability to change our lives. Scriptures are like seeds, as Jesus describes in many parables, and seeds grow! Likewise, the Word will grow in your heart, as it's a living Word, whereas my words, are just my words.

So here's my book, I pray that you will enjoy it, that it will help you in your goals and that through it, you may know Jesus a little more too.

1. WHAT ARE WE THINKING?

To start the process of being slim on the outside, we need to focus our thoughts and be slim on the inside:

Proverbs 23:7 As a man **thinketh** in his heart, so is he. (KJV)

> Everything we see, hear and feel started with a thought by someone at some time.

What we're thinking is such an important issue. Everything we see, hear and feel started with a thought by someone at some time and what we see in the mirror is a result of our thoughts. How can I say that? It says so in the scripture above. So, what and how are you thinking about yourself? What do you expect to see in the mirror? What do you think you look like? How do you feel about yourself?

We need to examine what we think about ourselves, do we have positive thoughts or negative ones? Do we have low opinions about ourselves? If we do, then these need to change, before our outside appearances or situations will.

You see the battle is fought and won in our minds. If we can picture ourselves being slim in our imaginations then it will give us the impetus to keep going for our goals, and we'll become them, because God's Word has promised it. One of the reasons I believe that I'm thin, is that I see myself as being thin in my head. For instance, when I was pregnant it used to shock me every time I looked in the mirror, because I still thought of myself as being thin. When I saw that my tummy protruded further than my toes it was a surprise, because in my head I'm thin, I see myself as being thin. I should imagine, you're thinking "It does shock me when I see myself in the mirror!" But does that shock you because you're "bigger" than you thought? We need to change our minds and meditate on being slim instead.

Every thought

Do you ever find yourself thinking, "I could eat all day?" or other such thoughts.

2 Corinthians 10:5 ... take captive **every thought** to make it obedient to Christ.

We need to train our brains so that **every thought** we have regarding our size, appetite and needs are in accordance to His Word. We need to train our heads, with regard to food; train them not to be hungry at the wrong times or when there's absolutely no need for it! I used to think that when I ate late, I would be starving the following morning ... and I was!! However now I've changed my way of thinking and guess what, I can now wake up perfectly normal. These, **'every thoughts'**, can be so subtle, and come at us unawares, so we always need to be vigilant and make sure each one lines up with the Word of God, so they work for us rather than against us.

A popular quote is, "You are what you eat." Do you believe that? Yes, we do need to be careful what we eat, some of the foods out there are just bad for us (such as sugar) but I don't believe we need to be ruled by it, because instead of us becoming our food; our food becomes us; and we are blessed by the Almighty.

Do we condemn ourselves?

Do we hurt ourselves further by condemning or punishing ourselves for the food we've eaten? Do you think Christ condemns us? Because He doesn't!

Romans 8:1 Therefore, there is now **no condemnation** for those who are in Christ Jesus, because through Christ Jesus the law of the Spirit of life set me free from the law of sin and death.

Here we see, that we need to make sure we're not thinking condemning thoughts about ourselves as well. A lot of years ago I went on a sun bed for nine minutes! As you can imagine it was far too long for someone who hadn't been on a sun bed for a decade and so I was in extreme pain for a few days afterwards. Now I believe, we're already healed as it says in:

1 Peter 2:24 By His wounds you **have been** healed.

But although I knew the Lord could, would and had healed me, because I felt it was my own fault, I didn't let Him, I felt that the pain I was suffering was just desserts for being so stupid. Now that was for only a few days and I'm sure you're all saying that was silly. I think the Lord did too! He didn't want me to be condemned at all, that's not what He died for, He died so that I might have **abundant** life and not be in pain, humiliation or suffering for any reason. So, if I could've let go of those condemning thoughts, I would've been healed, and that definitely makes more sense.

Do you think that you deserve to be big? Is there something in your life that you're punishing yourself for? Don't! Jesus has already forgiven you for it. He has already paid the price for whatever it is. He has taken your punishment, you don't have to take it as well. He doesn't want you to feel condemned, He wants you to have abundant life. Can you change anything now anyway? No. You have to move on. Think on your future and not on your past, and accept that He can heal you of being overweight and receive it.

What do we meditate on?

What is meditation? It's when we think, ponder and mull over something for a long time. What do we ponder about? What is our prevalent thought during the day? Do we have negative thoughts or are we thinking about scripture?

> Meditation is when we think, ponder and mull over something for a long time.

I really like the passage of scripture in Joshua 1 where God is telling Joshua not to be afraid or dismayed as he takes over the leadership, of the Israelites, from Moses. During it, He says:

Joshua 1:8 Do not let this Book of the Law depart from your mouth; **meditate** on it day and night, so that you may be careful to do everything written in it. Then you will be prosperous and successful.

Like Joshua, we need to stop thinking about our problems and instead think about God's promises from His Word, think on them day and night, and then we, like Joshua, will be successful too.

Matthew 6:25 Therefore I tell you, **do not worry** about your life, what you will eat or drink; or about your body what you will wear. Is not life more important than food, and the body more important than clothes?

V33 (goes on to say) But seek first His kingdom and His righteousness, and all these things will be given to you as well.

Worry is a form of negative thinking, negative meditation. How long do we worry about things? Ages! We can worry all the time, when we're working, feeding the kids, driving and ironing! But time spent worrying can be better spent elsewhere – like meditating on the Word. If we could study the scripture for as long as we worry about things, our lives would change. It would take our focus off our problems and onto the Lord and His righteousness, and then

> Time spent worrying can be better spent elsewhere.

our problems wouldn't even seem like problems! The Lord then goes onto say, by seeking His kingdom instead of worrying He will give us all the things we need anyway, which is so fantastic, I haven't the words for it!

Perception v reality

Optical illusions, are when we perceive something to be true to find out it's false. How many times have we perceived something incorrectly and the reality was actually something

> When we think and meditate on God we magnify Him and He dwarfs our problem.

else? I'm sure you've heard the saying, 'making a mountain out of a molehill!' When we think and meditate on a problem we magnify it, we make it bigger than it really is. When we think and meditate on God we magnify Him, He becomes bigger and more important to us, and He dwarfs our problem, making it small in comparison. And the great news is: He **IS** bigger than our problems. Let's put our focus on Jesus and then our weight, diet, food and any other problems we have, will be taken care of by Him!

Galatians 5:16 So I say, live by the Spirit, and you will not gratify the desires of the sinful nature.

That's it! That's all there is to it! We need to take our minds off our problems and put them onto the Spirit and live by it too, and then all those desires will not be gratified.

I was watching the television one day – I know what a confession - but I do sometimes! Anyway, as I was watching the television, the sun was streaming through the windows and casted a reflection of my garden on the screen. Now depending on what I concentrated on, depended on what I could see clearly. If I looked for the picture being transmitted I could see it plainly, likewise if I concentrated on the reflection, I saw my garden. This is the same in real life. If we concentrate on our problems, such as being overweight, then that's what we'll see, that's what we'll worry about. But if we can direct our thoughts to Christ, His love for us and think on how wonderfully we've been made, we'll have a totally different picture!

Feeling good

Remember no one "feels" good about themselves, we only have to look at magazine articles to realise that includes (what the world deems as) desirable people too. For myself there are a whole list of things I would change and I haven't met anyone who's any different. We'll never satisfy our lust for something different, and for some parts of us to change. If we looked like one beautiful person, we'd want to look like another. Let's stop that and instead meditate on positive things about ourselves, such as what and how God thinks about us. How do we find that out? We look in the bible, we read His words which are relevant to us here and now. Here are a couple of scriptures to start with.

Psalm 139:14 I praise You because I am fearfully and **wonderfully made**; Your works are wonderful, I know that full well.

Do we know that full well? Do we know that we're wonderfully made? What about this one?

Zephaniah 3:17 The Lord your God is with you, He is mighty to save, He will take **great delight** in you, He will quiet you with His love, He will **rejoice over you** with singing.

Jesus thinks we're so great, He takes great delight in us, He rejoices over us with singing! Wow!

And, here's a wonderful promise of the Lord:

Isaiah 26:3 You will keep in perfect peace, him whose **mind** is steadfast, because he trusts in You.

> We need to train our brains so that when they start wandering off down negative routes we think of God's goodness instead.

If we can just keep our minds focused on the Lord instead of our appetite, hunger, looks, what people think of us, weight and waistlines, then we'll have perfect peace. Wow! We need to train our brains so that when they start wandering off down those negative routes, we change course and instead, think of God's goodness and what He's done for us. In fact, at this moment let's just take some time to think on God. Think of His power, His creation, His love, His provision, His gentleness, His patience, His everything. Our God is truly magnificent and worthy of our time and thoughts.

Philippians 4:8 Whatsoever things are true, whatsoever things are noble, whatsoever things are just, whatsoever things are pure, whatsoever things are lovely, whatsoever things are of good report; if there be any virtue, and if there be any praise, **THINK** on these things. KJV)

You can see there's a vein running throughout the bible that explains the power of thoughts. We have a tendency, to overlook their value in everyday life, in the worldly scheme of things, but to God they're of the utmost importance and they DO have a huge impact over us. Instead then, we need to realise their significance and use them properly, to be wary of their destructive power and use them for our success not failure.

Going forward

Think about any bad perceptions you have and change them into good ones. Were you thin as a youngster? I want you to meditate on how you used to look, not in a self-piteous way but in a positive way, saying to yourself that you are going to look like that again – only more mature and beautiful!

Think about your thought processes – do you have any damaging ones – do you think you're hungry all the time, do you think of yourself as lazy? Take some time to analyse yourself, your thought processes and renew your mind to produce better results. Romans 12:2 says we need to have our minds **constantly** renewed, so don't do this just once either, it needs to be checked all the time.

I want you to meditate on what God thinks about you – you were made in His image, you were fearfully and wonderfully made by Him, this is the truth. I want

> You were made in His image, you were fearfully and wonderfully made by Him, this is the truth.

you to let the Lord renew your mind about yourself without feelings of condemnation getting in the way.

So, to end this chapter I have another challenge; fold a piece of paper in half, list all the negative thoughts you have about yourself on one side and then against each one write a positive scripture on the other side. Such as:

My bum is too big   "I am made in the image of Christ" Genesis 1:26

I can't lose weight   "I can do all things through Christ" Philippians 4:13

Then, tear up the negative list as a sign you're ready to change your mindset and keep the promises close by (maybe put them on a mirror) to remind yourself that you are "More than a conqueror" Romans 8:37 and "He will bring to completion every good work that was started in you." Philippians 1:6

2. WHAT ARE WE SAYING?

In the last chapter, we addressed what we thought about ourselves, so the next step is to find out what we are or have been **saying** about ourselves.

Matthew 12:34 For out of the overflow of the heart the mouth **speaks**.

Have you been saying what you are, only to find, you are what you say? Then you say what you are and so still are what you say? What we have to do is swap it around and decide how we want

> Have you been saying what you are, only to find, you are what you say?

to be and say what we want, so that we can have what we say!

Proverbs 18:21 The **tongue has the power of life and death**, and those who love it will eat its fruit.

When God created the world, He did so by speaking things into existence.

Genesis 1:3 And God **SAID** let there be light.

There is creative power in words, God spoke and God created. As we're made in His image, when we speak things out we are, in a way, creating things too. We need, therefore, to be careful what we're saying, as what we say can be constructive or

20

> ## How much does it cost to change your words? Nothing!

destructive. Have you heard the slogans, 'Name it and claim it,' 'Doubt it and do without it?' Well they're true, and His Word testifies to it again and again. So then, we need to put this into practice when it comes to slimming. Sounds really easy hey? Well it is! How much does it cost to change your words? Nothing!! How much energy do we need to put into speaking? None at all! So, let's start calling ourselves slim! We may look silly sometimes, or at least feel silly sometimes, but hey are we fools for Christ or not? It worked for Abraham, when he was childless, and so it'll work for us.

Romans 4:17 ... God Who gives life to the dead and calls things that are not as though they were.

What should we say then? Well, maybe first, we need to stop what we're currently saying! When Gabriel informed Zachariah he would have a child, Zachariah didn't believe it and was struck mute. Why? So that he wouldn't hinder the plans of God by speaking doubt. (Luke 1:5-20)

How many times have we said insulting things about ourselves in jest? Why? Is it from embarrassment? Is it to make a joke of a serious situation? We need to stop. We need to stop making excuses for ourselves and following the world's way and start speaking the truth from the Word of God. So, even though you aren't slim yet, start proclaiming that you are, you aren't lying; you're speaking in faith. Here's some of the things I say about

21

myself – you can copy them if you like, or make up new ones for yourself; I say, "I have a fast system; in fact, I don't need laxatives at all!" I also say, "I can eat anything I like and it won't affect my size." How many times have I heard other people say, "I only have to look at something and I put a pound on," – now that really is a shame!!

Ephesians 4:29 Do not let any **unwholesome talk** come out of your mouths, but only what is helpful for building others up according to their needs, that it may benefit those who **listen**.

You know the person who listens to us the most, is ourselves! We're always there when we're speaking! So, not only do we need to make sure that what we're saying is going to encourage others, but we also need to

> You know the person we listen to the most is ourselves!

make sure it's going to encourage ourselves too. Let's not put ourselves down, because even if it isn't true, we'll start to believe it. Instead let's build ourselves up with our words, and even if we don't believe them now – we will!

Having authority

When we're speaking in faith, don't just wish for it either, compromising by saying, "Oh I'd love to be slim," or "I wish I could be slim…" What would have happened if God had said, "I wish there would be birds and fish," or, "Wouldn't it be nice

22

if the skies and seas were filled?" And Jesus had said, "I wish I could raise Lazarus from the dead. Please Lazarus, if you can hear me, I pray you come back to life?" Nothing! Instead the Lord decided what He wanted in His mind and then spoke the words with authority, with conviction and with confidence. Notice He didn't use many words either, He kept it short. We should keep our declarations concise and to the point.

Matthew 6:7 And when you pray, do not keep on babbling like pagans, for they think they will be heard because of their **many words**.

Let's see what Jesus said when He raised Lazarus from the dead; "Lazarus, come forth." Just three words, but what power! We don't need to shout or stamp our feet either. We have authority, Jesus has given us the right, to use His Name, the Name that's above all names – even the name of "fat", of "obesity" ALL NAMES. So, let's use it!

> Jesus is the Name that is above all names – even the name of "Fat."

Mark 11:22-23 "Have faith in God," Jesus answered. "I tell you the truth, if anyone **says** to this mountain, 'Go throw yourself into the sea,' and does not doubt in his heart but believes that what he **says** will happen, **IT WILL BE DONE FOR HIM.**"

What is the mountain? It's whatever we feel our problems to be, maybe it's our bodies, food addictions or something else. We

23

need to use what the Lord has given us, tongues, to speak and 'move our mountains,' and when we believe that it will happen, **it will be done for us**.

We also need to speak to the actual mountain – not other people about the mountain, not to God about the mountain, but to the mountain. We need to address our problems by speaking directly to them.

> We need to speak to our mountains.

So, let's speak to our fat, whether it be on our stomachs, thighs or bingo wings! Tell it to go, in the Name of Jesus. Then, "not doubt in our hearts" as we need to believe in what we say.

What are we hearing?

Romans 10:17 So then faith cometh by **hearing**, and hearing by the word of God. (KJV)

If we are speaking, we are also hearing and listening. A while ago part of my job entailed hearing sales pitches about kitchens. I didn't need a kitchen, I didn't want a kitchen, but I was getting paid to listen to sales advisors all day. By the end of eight hours though, I wanted one! Listening to something, over and over again, can change the way we think, and what we think!

Hearing the Word of God is even more powerful than salesmen, there seems to be a chemical reaction that happens when hearing the Word takes place. It's like a formula in physics or maths.

> Hearing + Word of God = Faith

Hearing + Word of God = Faith. We can

24

hear other people speak the Word, but it's even better when we speak the Word of God to ourselves, as faith is created as a by-product. Likewise, if all we're hearing is negative words about ourselves, then those will be the ones we believe instead.

Faith

What is faith? You may be asking at this point. Let's find out what it says in the bible:

Hebrews 11:1 Now faith is **being sure** of what we hope for and certain of what we do not see.

What are we hoping for? We need to be sure and certain that we have it and see ourselves, as we will be, even though we don't see it yet.

> We need to be sure that we have, what we hope for, and see ourselves as we will be.

It then goes on to say:

Hebrews 11:6 But without faith it is impossible to please Him, for he that cometh to God must believe that He is, and that He is a rewarder of them that diligently seek Him. (KJV)

First, we see in this verse that by having faith we'll be pleasing God – that's good news for a start! Then we need to believe that He is. He is what? That He is God, that He is mighty (to do all things), He is the creator, the Supreme Being of the whole cosmos. Second, that He rewards us! Notice that this is in the present tense, so we'll be rewarded straight away! Why? Because He's full of love for us.

1 John 4:8 For God **is love**.

John 16:27 The Father Himself **loves you**, because you have loved me and have believed that I came from God.

So, because He loves us, He's only going to do good things towards us and He doesn't want to hurt or trap us.

At the end of the verse it says, "that He is a rewarder of them that diligently seek Him," the only pre-requisite, for our rewards, is that we diligently seek him! – which means: search out, investigate, crave, demand, worship, en-(re)-quire, seek after carefully.[1] It doesn't say that we have to do everything correctly without making any mistakes, thankfully. Instead we just need to search out God, crave Him and worship Him.

> What then starts off as words, will start to become realities.

What then starts off as words, will start to become realities, even if we still can't physically see, hear, touch, feel or taste them. Because, when it comes to the point where we seem to stop "believing" for them and instead

---

[1] Ekseteo Taken from e-sword, who takes it from Strong's Hebrew and Greek dictionaries, G1537 and G2212

26

"know" that we have them, then that is faith; being "certain of what we do not see." (Hebrews 11:1)

Going back and carrying on from Romans 4:17 regarding Abraham, where it says; "Calls things that are not, as though they were," the passage gives us some more great tips on how to use our faith and have our hopes manifest.

Romans 4:18-21 Who against hope **believed in hope**, that he might become the father of many nations, according to that which was spoken, "So shall thy seed be." And being not weak in faith, he **considered not** his own body now dead, when he was about a hundred years old, neither yet the deadness of Sarah's womb: **He staggered not** at the promise of God through unbelief; but was **strong in faith**, giving glory to God; And being **fully persuaded**, that what He had promised, He was able also to perform. (KJV)

There are really strong phrases and actions here that we can use: Are we hoping against hope? Are we considering our bodies – because we shouldn't! Are we staggering at the promises of God through unbelief? Are we strong in faith? Are we still giving glory to God? And, are we fully persuaded that God is able to help us?

The only thing we're really asked to do is believe, believe in Him, believe in His power and His loving nature, that He wants to help us. That's our work! That's all we have to do!

> The only thing we're asked to do is believe.

27

John 6:28-29 Then they asked Him, "What must we do to do the works God requires?" Jesus answered, "The work of God is this: to **believe** in the One He has sent."

Let's speak to our bodies then, with the knowledge that the Father is on our side, and tell them how we want them to behave, let's use the creative power God has given us to reduce our sizes instead of increasing them!! Let's speak with authority and power. The authority and power Jesus gave to us, when He defeated the devil on our behalf, and then this will help our belief too.

What do others say?

What have other people said about us as well? If we have creative power in our tongues, then other people – who are also made in the image of Christ – do too! Were you ridiculed at school? Were you given a nickname? Have you been labelled as fat? We can't change other people but we can change the response we give them. We can make a stand against them, speak in the name of Jesus and curse those curses to hell! We can start again, we don't need to be bound by those words any longer. Now, if anyone curses you again, say something to contradict it – the Word of God is best, such as – "I'm fearfully and wonderfully made." (Psalm 139:14) Use the sword of the Spirit (Word of God) to fight the words of the devil.

For instance, when I was pregnant many people; family and friends mainly (can't remember any enemies saying these things!) said things like, "I can't wait to see you fat!!" "I put on all my weight once I had kids – I bet you'll be the same!" But I always said something to counteract them, such as "Oh no I won't, I'll lose the weight don't you worry, I won't put on more weight than I need to." And as far as I can tell, it worked!

We can come against these curses that people have lovingly put on us and they don't have to harm us anymore, because the Lord became the curse for us.

> We can come against curses people have lovingly put on us.

Galatians 3:13 Christ redeemed us from the curse of the law, **by becoming a curse for us**: for it is written, "Cursed is everyone who is hung on a tree."

Accept this truth, and those words that have been said in the past cannot affect your present or future any more.

Take care!

Proverbs 18:7 A fool's **mouth** is his destruction, and his lips are the snare of his soul. (KJV)

We can't be fools, like it says here, we always need to be careful what we're saying and speak good things. Say that we're going to lose weight and that we're going to be the size we want.

Another useful portion of scripture is James 3:1-13; James says our tongues are like rudders on ships – even though ships are large, they're directed by small rudders, and likewise even though our tongues are small, compared to the rest of our bodies, they can direct our whole lives. James is very blunt about this subject, but don't get despondent, just remember that any change will make a big impact, it just helps to realise exactly how powerful our words/ tongues are.

Psalm 34: 12-13 What man is he who desires life and longs for many days, that he may see good? **Keep your tongue from evil** and your lips from speaking deceit. (Amp)

If we want to see good things and have long lives then we need to stop speaking negatively, pessimistically and sarcastically. We need to stop complaining, moaning and groaning and instead rejoice, in what God has given us. Rejoice, because we can have what we hope for. We can trust God, that He will reward us for whatever we hope for, why? Is it because of anything we have done? No, it's because of Jesus and His love. He has provided the way for us, He has defeated our enemy, He has given us tongues to speak with authority, so let's use them!

> He has provided the way for us, He has defeated our enemy.

Going forward

So first of all, I would say the best thing you can do is be quiet! Stop speaking negatively about yourselves. Instead, here are some great scriptures that you can speak out, to start the process of calling those things which are not as though they were.

(Romans 4:17) They're taken from different translations of the bible; KJV, Amplified and NIV. A lot have already been mentioned in this book but I've changed the wording slightly to make them easy to say and personal. Say them every day, they really can make a difference!

Genesis 1:26 I am made in God's image.

Joshua 1:8 I will not let the Word out of my mouth and will meditate on it day and night, so that my way will be prosperous, I will deal wisely and have good success.

Psalm 23:1 The Lord is my Shepherd, (to feed, guide and shield me), I shall not lack.

Psalm 23:6 Only goodness, mercy and unfailing love shall follow me all the days of my life.

Psalm 34:8-10 The Lord is good. I am blessed because I take refuge in Him. I will respect His wisdom and Word and so will lack nothing. I will seek the Lord and so lack no good thing.

Psalm 37:4 I will delight myself in the Lord and He will give me the desires of my heart.

Psalm 103:1-5 I will praise the Lord, He has forgiven my sin, He has healed every disease, He has redeemed my life, He has crowned me with love and compassion, He has satisfied my desires with good things and my youth is renewed like the eagles.

Psalm 139:14 I am fearfully and wonderfully made.

Proverbs 3:5-8 I will trust the Lord with all my heart and lean not on my own understanding but in all my ways I will acknowledge Him and He will make my paths straight. I will not be wise in my own eyes, but fear the Lord and resist evil; this will bring health to my body and nourishment to my bones.

Proverbs 4:20-22 I attend to His Words, consent and submit to His sayings, I will not let them depart from my sight and will keep them in the centre of my heart. They are life to me, healing and health to my flesh.

Proverbs 16:3 I will commit my works to the Lord and trust Him with them, He will cause my thoughts to become agreeable to His will and so shall the plans be established and succeed.

Zechariah 4:6 It isn't by my might or my strength but by His Spirit.

Matthew 6:31,33 I will not worry about what I'm eating, drinking or wearing because the Lord knows that I need them. But I will seek His kingdom and His righteousness and all these things will be given to me.

> **Make these scriptures part of your daily diet**

Mark 11:23 I will speak to the mountains in my life and not doubt that what I say will take place and what I say will be done for me.

Romans 8:37,39 I am more than a conqueror through Jesus who loves me. For nothing will separate me from His love.

Romans 12:1-2 I will present my body as a living sacrifice. I will not mould into the pattern of this world but I will be transformed by the renewing of my mind. I will then be able to test and approve what God's will is – His good, pleasing and perfect will.

2 Corinthians 10:5 I will demolish arguments and every pretension that sets itself up against the knowledge of God and take captive every thought to make it obedient to Christ.

Galatians 5:16 I will walk and live in the Spirit (responsive to and controlled and guided by the Spirit) then I will not gratify the cravings and desires of my flesh.

Ephesians 3:20 Jesus, by the Holy Spirit that is at work within me, is able to carry out His purpose and do superabundantly, far over and above all that I dare to ask or think, infinitely beyond my highest prayers, desires, thoughts, hopes or dreams.

Philippians 1:6 Jesus who began a good work in me will carry it on to completion until the day of Christ Jesus.

Say them every day they really make a difference!

Philippians 4:13 I can do all things through Christ who strengthens me.

Hebrews 10:23 I will seize and hold fast and retain without wavering the hope I cherish and confess and my acknowledgement of it, for He who promised is reliable and faithful to His Word.

Hebrews 13:5 God has said, I will not in any way fail …. (insert own name), nor give up, nor leave … (insert own name) without support. I will not, I will not, I will not leave … (insert own name) helpless nor forsaken nor let … (insert own name) down, relax my hold on … (insert own name) Assuredly not!

Revelation 4:11 God is worthy to receive all glory, honour and power, for He has created all things, and for His pleasure I was created.

Make these scriptures your daily diet and your life will change! Find some more to add to them or make a list of your own. But use scriptures, as they are the most powerful words there are. Jesus referred to His Words as seeds – and they have the power to germinate and bring life!

3. WHY ARE WE EATING?

I've found two reasons for eating in the bible; to stay alive and to fellowship or celebrate. Elijah was kept alive by ravens bringing him food every day, (1 Kings 17) and the Israelites were given manna in the desert. (Exodus 16) So the Lord understands we need food to sustain our bodies and provides this for us.

With regards to celebrations, these are found throughout the Old Testament, (the Passover for instance) and there were countless times in the New Testament when Jesus and His apostles got together and broke bread too. Although do be aware, it's easy to fool ourselves into thinking we're celebrating all the time. If we're constantly fellowshipping – we'll have to say, "No thank you," sometimes!!! This is a trap I found myself falling into; when I had my little boy, I was always at friends' houses, so that the children could play together, or going out for lunch. I was eating so much lovely food, biscuits and cakes, I didn't realise my waist line was extending to accommodate it! So, there has to be wisdom and we need to take control of our habits before they control us!

> Be aware! It's easy to think we're celebrating all the time. We'll have to say, "No," sometimes!

So, getting back to the main question of why do **we** eat? There are many reasons and let's consider some of these now and find ways of approaching them in a different manner, so that food won't be the answer to them anymore. Instead God will.

35

Hunger? Well, it certainly feels like a really good reason to eat! However, we're then just letting our bodies do the talking. Now this is going to sound harsh, but Philippians 3:19 speaks about our gods being our stomachs. Our stomachs want control! They want to master our whole bodies and be our gods, but we can't let them! We can't let our stomachs be our gods, we can't let our stomachs rule our heads.

> Our bodies are like children, if we give them an inch they will take a mile!

Our bodies are like children – our stomachs especially, if we give them an inch they'll take a mile. We've always got to be in control of them. But just like children, they'll learn to take correction and understand that, "No, really means, No!" If we're firm and consistent, that is.

Hunger can be deceiving too. Is it really hunger or is it appetite? What we need to consider is; when did we last have a meal? How much did we eat? What have we done since? If the answers to these are; not very long ago, a fry up and watched television – then how can we be truly hungry? It's just an illusion. Just say "No!" – because if we don't, they'll try and trick us again and again. We have to be firm with our stomachs until they get the hint that we aren't going to put up with their lies any longer.

Ecclesiastes 6:7 All the labour of man is for his mouth, and yet the **appetite is not filled**.

Our appetites can feel like hunger. They can be so realistic. But like this verse says, have we been able to satisfy our appetites yet? If we do, do we not feel absolutely stuffed as a result? Personally, I don't get much of a warning, from when I think, "I can still eat," to when, "I'm overflowing!" Those, 'All-you-can-eat' restaurants are awful for me, my eyes are definitely, 'bigger than my belly.' And do they really make me feel better when I've indulged myself so much? No. I've always regretted them. So, we need to eat with wisdom. Eat with our heads and not our appetites. We need to decide how much we're going to have and stick to it. If we go to a buffet, just have one plate. Enjoy what we have, but then stop! Appetites will always fancy something, they will always desire more. The only way to stop these appetites, is not to give into them. Say, "No." Say, "No," again, and then they'll finally stop asking! They'll give up! And, it won't take forever, honestly.

OK confession time! I've never completely stopped my appetite, and I have given into my stomach. When this happens though, it doesn't take long before my appetite thinks it has a hold on me again. So, I have to be constantly vigilant, and repeat the process, and you will too. We need to take each day as a new beginning and say, "No," to them again. The second time is always easier than the first, because you know you'll win, we always win!

> Take each day as a new beginning.

Because we don't think it'll make any difference? Do you believe that you're so big now, it won't matter if you have an extra bite? Or that you've eaten so much already today, that it won't make any difference? That you completely pigged out yesterday, so you might as well give up for the week? Don't let those thoughts fool you, every time you say, "No," to yourself you're winning a battle in your head and over your body. Every calorie you refuse, is a calorie less to burn off – you're doing well – keep it up! Every single sweet, spoon of sugar, mouthful of cake and chip makes a difference. Congratulate yourself that you were able to say, "No," that you were able to leave it on your plate, that you were able to put it in the rubbish. You're really doing well. The more praise we give ourselves, the more confident we'll be and the less of a hold food will have on us.

Because it's time to eat? So, when our bodies aren't telling us to eat - our brains are!!! Do you really think we need to eat three meals, plus snacks every day? Has anyone in history eaten so much, so often? I've read and seen many news reports saying we need at least five portions of fruit and vegetables, three portions of dairy foods, then carbohydrates, then fibre, then protein, then omega 3 every day. I sometimes think if I ate everything they said I needed to survive, I'd never stop eating!

> Sometimes, I think if I ate everything the news reports said I needed to survive, I would never stop eating!

Ever! Now, we have to show some sense in this, if we aren't going to listen to our stomachs or our brains at all, we would starve – we do have to eat sometimes. But, if you're not hungry and it's lunchtime, just don't have anything! If you've made sandwiches stick them in the fridge, they may keep until tomorrow, worst comes to the worst you may have to throw them away or feed them to the ducks! If you aren't hungry at breakfast

38

– don't have it! If you need to get your metabolism going, run up and down the stairs a few times! If you need to take medication with food, see if you can have it with just a piece of fruit instead. Anyway, let's use wisdom, but I think you can see the point I'm making – don't eat just because of the time.

Because it's there? I was brought up in a home where no food was wasted at all, if I didn't have all my dinner, I was told I would have it for breakfast! Then, when I went to boarding school, I just ate everything in sight! Pretty much! As I could never be sure how much food I would get the following day. However, I don't live in those conditions any more. And the excuses that we can all come up with, are probably null and void now, as we lead independent lives. So how are we going to combat them? Well, the obvious thing; is to not buy the offending food, in the first place! If it's not there, then we can't be tempted by it! Plan what you're going to eat and don't buy anything else (it'll also help with the weekly budget.) Avoid aisles that sell the products that don't contain any nutritional value – you know the ones. Cook smaller portions, only put what you need on your plate, save any left-overs for the following day, or, just throw them away.

We live in an age where billions of pounds' worth of food gets thrown away every year and although I don't advocate wastage, sometimes it's necessary. I heard recently of a diet where you just eat half of everything! You can have anything you like as long as you only eat half of it – there would be a lot of wastage in that, but it's a quick way of halving your calorie intake.

Contrary to what I've just written though, I'm one of those people who wants what they **can't** have! I **can** have chocolate in my cupboard for months and finally have to throw it away! But as soon as I don't have any "nice things" available, I want them! So, for me I always have crisps, chocolate and sweets in stock and they last for months and sometimes years! You know yourself better than I do – so you know what you need to do!

Boredom? This is a tricky one – how any of us gets bored, is quite amazing, when we don't have time to turn around some days!! It's funny when our eyes and ears are being so stimulated by the television, radio, advertising, mobile phones and computers, and our touch sense is being aroused by our comforts, the softness of our sofas, the firmness of our beds (everything is comfortable isn't it?) that we can still get bored! What a pity our senses of smell and taste are also craving gratification, as

> How do we get bored when our senses are stimulated so much?

well as our eyes, ears and touch. But they do! What we need, is to find other things to pass the time. A definition of 'bored' in the Oxford Living dictionary is: "Feeling weary and impatient because one is unoccupied or lacks interest in one's current activity."[2] It makes me wonder whether these diversions – television, radio, computers etc. are really exciting? Surely if they were, we wouldn't be bored, would we?

As I've said before, our bodies are like children – except they never grow up! A good way of soothing a child when they're upset, is diverting them, and we can use the same tactic on our flesh! So, what can we do to divert ourselves? Enjoy what else life has to offer. I'm sure the Lord won't mind if we use Him as

---

[2] Oxford Living Dictionary 26/04/16 15:10

> **Feed our spirits with the Word of God instead of our bodies.**

a way to divert ourselves. Put on a praise tape and have a song and dance – not only will this fill the boredom, but it'll also release endorphins that'll make us feel better. Reading the Word of God would also help – feeding our spirits instead of our bodies, enjoy a pastime, take up a hobby, write a book! There are so many ideas, what have you always wanted to do? Do anything but put the television on, or the radio – not only are they probably the reasons why we're bored in the first place, but they're also full of adverts and images of food that are deliberately made to tempt you – otherwise they wouldn't be on there would they?

Psalm 46:10 Be still and know I am God.

Being still is not very popular in our society, but the bible clearly advocates it! When we're bored maybe we should just sit still, instead of reaching for the remote control or opening the fridge door. Maybe we should just think on God. I wonder how much our lives would change if we did that! I know for certain they would improve. I'm sure they would become more interesting and exciting. Our Lord certainly led an exciting life, as did the apostles after Him and He wants us to have interesting, exciting and productive lives too, just like them.

Stress? Personally, in times of mega stress, I lose weight –such as when my first husband left me. But, things can easily go the other way too. Normal, everyday stress can make us feel low and needing food, let alone major life-changing, stressful events. How can we combat these stressful times? One way, is just by taking time out of our day to spend with the Lord, to feel His love and care for us. Taking time out of the hustle and bustle and being quiet and still.

After God made the earth He rested. Do we spend enough time resting? Just relaxing? Originally God ordained the Sabbath to be a holy day and for His people to have time off. Was that just so that He could be a control freak? So, He could tell people what to do? Or do you think it was because humans actually needed rest? I watched an interview with an Olympian a little while ago. They were chatting about their training schedule. Guess what? They train all day, every day for six days and then do nothing on the seventh!! Totally nothing! If they need time off, so do we! We need time to unwind. To de-stress ourselves.

If you are stressed because, 'the only person you can trust is yourself.' Don't be deceived, we can trust God! And who are we compared to Him. He knows way more than we can ever imagine, so let's not trust ourselves but Him. We are not told in the bible to trust others either – they'll only let us down, if not straight away, then eventually.

Proverbs 3 5-8, **Trust in the Lord** with all your heart and lean **not** on your own understanding; in all your ways acknowledge Him and He will make your paths straight. Do not be wise in our own eyes; fear the Lord and shun evil. This will bring health to your body and nourishment to your bones.

Jesus is the One Who we can trust. He is the one Who knows the end from the beginning. He knows what's best for us. We just need to respond to His guidance. We need to listen to His instruction. Jesus will always be there for us and will never fail us.

Depression? Life can be pretty mundane sometimes, working, sleeping and looking after everyone else can leave us feeling run down and washed up. Food is an easy comfort – it doesn't take much time and it makes us immediately feel better. But there are long-term effects to food, as we know, so what else can we do? One solution I found, was when I was working as a temp – I didn't feel any good to anyone at the time, and I was low. I wanted to cheer myself up – so I bought some flowers – they really did the job, not only did they cheer my office up, they lasted a long time and didn't make me feel guilty afterwards. Another time, I took myself to my bedroom, put some really good tunes on and danced! I danced like crazy! It was a good job I was alone! But oh, it did make me feel better! The Lord can also fill this gap, spend some time with Him. Even if it's the length of time it takes to eat a chocolate bar, don't eat the chocolate bar, just sit back, close your eyes and think of His love.

> Spend some time with the Lord, even if it's just the time it takes to eat a chocolate bar.

But are we feeling depressed from some other, deeper issue? Do we feel loved? Do we have self-worth? Are we lonely? Are we experiencing grief? If we are, we definitely need to be thinking and meditating on God's love, provision, grace and mercy, so that we can fully overcome these things.

Psalm 103:17 From everlasting to everlasting the **Lord's love** is with those who fear Him.

Isaiah 54:10 "Though the mountains be shaken and the hills be removed, yet **My unfailing love** for you will not be shaken nor My covenant of peace be removed" says the Lord who has compassion on you.

Romans 8:38-39 For I am convinced that neither death nor life, neither angels or demons, neither the present nor the future, nor any powers, neither height nor depth, nor anything else in all creation, **will be able to separate us from the love of God that is in Christ Jesus our Lord.**

1 Corinthians 13:4-8 **Love is** patient, love is kind. It does not envy, it does not boast, it is not proud. It is not rude, it is not self-seeking, it is not easily angered, it keeps no record of wrongs. Love does not delight in evil but rejoices with the truth. It always protects, always trusts, always hopes, always perseveres. Love never fails.

As God is love (1John 4:8) **this is how He feels about us.** He loves us and that same love lives inside us, so that we can love back! He's not a cat or dog, (although these are wonderful and can be great sources of joy and companionship) He's not even just a man. He is **God!** The One Who is eternal. The One Who created the earth and sky! And He loves us! All the time! He is with us, all the time! Our self-worth should not be a problem if we can get to grips with this!

If it's grief please be reassured that:

2 Peter 3:9 ... He is patient with you, not wanting **anyone to perish** .....

The Lord does not want anyone to perish or die instead:

John 10:10 The thief comes only to steal and **kill** and destroy; I come that they may have **life**, and have it to the full.

Jesus came to give us life and He gave us the Holy Spirit, who comforts us. So, if this is an issue for you, please don't think the Lord took the person away from you and let Him help you instead. Let Him comfort you.

John 14:16 And I will ask the Father, and He will give you another **Comforter** (Counsellor, Helper, Intercessor, Advocate, Strengthener and Standby), that He may remain with you forever. (Amp)

And, in relation to loneliness:

Hebrews 13:5 (latter half in the Amplified): He (God) Himself has said, I will not in any way fail you nor give you up, **nor leave you without support**. (I will) not, (I will) not, (I will) not in any degree leave you helpless nor forsake nor let (you) down (relax My hold on you) (Assuredly not!)

If we can wrap our heads around how much Jesus loves us, wants us and has done for us then we should never be depressed again! He gave His life for us! God gave His only begotten son for us!

> If we can wrap our heads around how much Jesus loves us, we should never be depressed again!

Revelation 4:11 Thou are worthy, O Lord, to receive glory and honour and power: for thou hast created all things, and for **thy pleasure** they are and were created. (NKJV)

We have been created for God's pleasure! He delights in us! So even if you can't love yourself, at the moment, let Jesus love you.

The other stuff!

Do we have feelings of unforgiveness, anger, disappointment, hurt or bitterness? Again, just realising our worth in Christ can deliver us from these. And, if we meditate on what He accomplished on the cross we'll see that not only were our sins placed on Him, but so were the sins of everyone else in the world. Everyone who has ever hurt us, let us down or deliberately wronged us; has had their punishment taken by

Jesus. He's paid the price for their crimes, thoughtlessness and sometimes downright stupidity, as well as ours! Should we then punish them (or ourselves, by-proxy) any further?

In the Amplified version of **Isaiah 53:4-5**, the text explains exactly what Jesus took from us on the cross: **Surely He has borne our grief's, (sicknesses, weaknesses and distresses) and carried our sorrows and pains (of punishment).** And with the stripes (that wounded) Him we are healed and made whole.

There doesn't need to be a deliverance service, we don't need to have hands placed on us, we can change these feelings by ourselves and the Holy Spirit! Just meditate on what He has done for us and get into the Word of God! Let those feelings go and let the Holy Spirit heal us!

The Holy Spirit wants to help!

> The Holy Spirit will help, He is our comforter, counsellor and teacher.

I have mentioned the Holy Spirit a few times now. He is the third part of the Godhead. He is wonderful and He's here to help us too. He's our comforter, our counsellor, our teacher. He guides us into all truth and He tells us the will of God. If you don't have the Holy Spirit living in you right now, and you would like Him to, it just takes a simple prayer to Jesus. Pray that He will baptise you in the Holy Spirit. Jesus will never withhold anything good from you and so He will do as you ask. When the Holy Spirit came to live in me, it didn't feel strange or weird. I didn't feel possessed or crazy. Instead, I felt and still feel, a complete sense of love and support. He doesn't make me do anything I don't want to do, He's always with me and I have a deeper connection with the Father and Jesus, through Him.

With the help of the Holy Spirit, many of the things we're striving for, are a lot easier to obtain; as it's Him working through us, that overcomes all things. (Look up John 14 and John 16 for more information on the Holy Spirit.)

One of the manifestations of the Spirit is speaking in tongues. Note, it's not thinking in tongues but speaking. If you have asked for the gift of tongues and nothing came to mind, it might be because you need to utter some words (or rather sounds) first and then the Holy Spirit takes over and speaks for you. Tongues are amazing and quite often underestimated. When we don't know what to say, the Spirit speaks for us and does so in accordance with God's will (Romans 8:26-27) so we don't have to worry about what we're going to say! Tongues also edify

> Tongues are amazing and often underestimated.

us (which means to build us up), bring us joy and reveal the mysteries of God, and these verses prove it!

1 Corinthians 14:4 He who speaks in a (strange) tongue **edifies and improves himself**. (Amp)

Jude :20 But ye, beloved, **building up yourselves** on your most holy faith, praying in the Holy Ghost. (KJV)

Romans 8:26-27 In the same way, the Spirit helps us in our weakness. We do not know what we ought to pray for, but the Spirit Himself intercedes for us with groans that words cannot express. And He who searches our hearts knows the mind of the Spirit, because the Spirit intercedes for the saints in **accordance with God's will**.

1 Corinthians 2:10 and 13 But God has revealed it to us by His Spirit. The Spirit searches all things, even the deep things of God. This is what we speak, not in words taught us by human wisdom but in words taught by the Spirit, **expressing spiritual truths in spiritual words**.

Going forward

So, from now on, I want you to ask yourself whenever you're eating, "Why?" Is it for a genuine reason – are you practising hospitality? Do you need it to survive? Or, is it just appetite, time of day, boredom, stress or depression?

If it's for any of those latter reasons, try meditating on what God has done for you instead and how God feels about you.

I have said this before but I will say it again! Read and think on the scriptures that have been given:

John 6:63 The Spirit gives life; the flesh counts for nothing. The Words I have spoken to you are spirit and they are life.

Declare them aloud and you'll find that a reaction takes place. And instead of having to strive to change, it will happen effortlessly from the inside out.

If you don't have the Holy Spirit living inside you, or you don't speak in tongues, and you want to, ask Jesus and He will baptise you with them. This is what John the Baptist said:

Luke 3:16 John answered them all, "I baptise you with water. But one more powerful than I will come, the thongs of whose sandals I am not worthy to untie. **He will baptise you** with the **Holy Spirit** and with fire."

2 Corinthians 1:20 For all the promises of God in Him are Yes, and in Him Amen, to the glory of God through us. (NKJV)

And, at the end of the day, the answer to all our problems is Jesus, who never fails us. Jesus, Jesus, Jesus.

4. WHAT ARE WE EATING?

This is a book about slimming, and even though I don't want to, I have to tackle what we eat, at some point. I won't be telling anyone what to, or not to eat though, I will just give guidelines, as it says in Romans 14, we should not judge one another on what we eat.

First of all, I'll tell you my sad story! I'm being a little ironic as you'll find out as you read on! My first experience of '*having*' to lose weight occurred when I worked, as a dancer, on the cruise ships, ahh poor me! (I knew I'd make you feel sorry for me!) Well there was a clause in my contract to say I couldn't put on more than four pounds at any time (there was another clause that said I couldn't lose more than four pounds either – but my agent said that didn't apply to me!) If I did, I would have been fined, and worst-case scenario, fired. See I told you it was a very sad story!

OK so you may be laughing at how ridiculous that sounds, but for me, at that time, it was a disaster. My agent told me I had to lose weight to keep my job! My dream job! So,

> **When you have to lose weight, it becomes the focus of your life, and it became mine.**

I'm sure you can testify with me, that when you **have** to lose weight, it becomes the focus of your entire life. And it became mine. All I could think about was food! All I talked about was food. All day, all night, when I was working, when I was sleeping, all I thought about, was food.

What made it even harder, on the cruise ship, was that there were plenty of luxurious things to eat, and when I say plenty, I mean plenty! Breakfast, mid-morning snacks, lunch, afternoon tea, dinner and midnight pizza! All cooked for me, without any clearing up to do after! Well to cut a long story short, I found keeping my weight within this limit, impossible.

So, as I was meditating on my plight for the umpteenth time, (actually seeking the Lord about the answer, rather than just wishing I could have another piece of pizza or baklava) I felt the Lord tell me it was actually fizzy pop that was my problem. Before I went on the ship, I would just drink either water or coffee, but there, I could drink any soft drink I wanted, for free! It was summer, I was on the Mediterranean and it was hot! I drank loads of them! But when I cut the fizz out of my diet – I just drank either coffee or water – I was able to stick to my ideal weight with ease. Thank you, Lord!

What's your key to losing weight? Maybe it's fizzy pop, maybe it's something else? I don't know, but I do know Who does know, so ask Him!

What's your key?

James 1:5 If any of you lacks **wisdom**, he should ask God, who gives generously to all without finding fault, and it will be given to him.

John 14:14: You may ask Me for anything in My Name, and **I will do it**.

Matt 7:7: **Ask** and it will be given to you.

Now of course, I could've chosen not to listen to the prompting of the Holy Spirit, I could've thought I was mistaken, but I didn't. I listened and obeyed, I gave up fizzy drinks and rarely have one, even now. And, instead of feeling I've lost something - in that I can't drink what I want - I focus on the fact, that I can stay the weight I want. I remain positive and cheerful in my obedience. So, what's the moral of this story? Ask Jesus what your key is and give Him time to answer you. He will, He has promised to, you've just got to listen, wait, (that's the hardest part) trust what He says is true and then do it. This scripture confirms what I've said:

> Ask Jesus what your key is and give Him time to answer you. He will.

James 2:17 Faith by itself, if it is not accompanied by **action**, is dead.

Faith, is believing that what we hear from God is true and then the action is obeying it.

This is not an isolated incident, as the Lord has given me answers to other diet questions, on other occasions. A friend of mine had a lot of difficulty going to the toilet, whilst they were on a well-known diet. I felt the prompting of the Lord for weeks, before I was brave enough to suggest to my friend, that it was the rice based cereal they were eating every morning that was the culprit. However, once I obeyed the Lord and they responded, their trouble stopped. They have since restarted eating the cereal and maybe because they have stopped the rest of the diet, I don't know, but their system is still perfectly functional.

Our relationship with the Lord is a two-way thing: Our part is to ask the Lord for help, listen to His answer and then obey Him. His part, is that He knows us intimately, completely. He knows we're individual, more than just average. That we're unique, not normal and He will give us the answer that we personally need – it may not be the same answer as mine – in fact it probably won't be, but it will be the answer that will change your battle into a victory. That will bring you peace. He's the one who knows us inside out – He knows us better than we know ourselves! Do you know how many hairs there are on your head? Well unless you're bald or have far too much time on your hands I'm sure the answer is, "No," – but He does! If He knows such a personal, intimate detail about us like that, then surely, He will also know what we need to do, to be our ideal, healthy weight.

> He knows we are unique and He will give us the answer, that will change our battle into a victory.

Whilst you're waiting for the answers to the questions you have for Him though, some of this advice and information may be of interest:

Fizzy Drinks

So, let's find out about fizzy drinks and possibly why God told me to stay away from them. Well it seems, the main problem with them, is the amount of sugar they contain. According to the

NHS website[3] adults shouldn't have more than 30g of sugar per day, which is the equivalent of 7.5 teaspoons. However, in Pepsi, Red Bull and 7Up there is 11g per 100ml and in Coca Cola 10.6g.[4] This means in one 330ml can of Pepsi you have 36.3g of sugar and in Coca Cola 34.98g. Both therefore, have a lot more than the daily allowance, and that's just for one can!

Sugar, is also very addictive. According to a David Wolfe website[5] an experiment was carried out on rats, and 94% of them chose sugar as opposed to Cocaine! So, although it's a very good idea to cut out sugar there may be side effects if you do. However, I reckon these would be worth it in the long run, as I don't like the idea of being addicted to anything.

There are, of course, diet substitutes which contain sweetener instead of sugar, but I am loath to suggest these, as there's a lot of conflicting advice about whether they're good for you or not. Aspartame seems to be the most controversial. Most of the main brands contain this, whilst the home brands don't, so try those.

Please don't get too worried about this though, the Lord has even made provision for sugar and sweeteners:

Mark 16:18 and when they **drink deadly poison**, it will not hurt them at all.

---

[3] http://www.nhs.uk/Livewell/Goodfood/Pages/sugars.aspx 07/09/2017 14:00
[4] http://www.bbc.co.uk/news/magazine-35831125 07/09/2017 14:07
[5] https://www.davidwolfe.com/study-sugar-more-addictive-cocaine/ 07/09/2017 14:25

However, if you feel led to stop drinking and eating anything that contains sugar or Aspartame, then do.

Milk and Honey

These are great alternatives to fizzy drinks and sugar. I often replace the sugar in my coffee (I take one teaspoon) for honey, when I have the beginnings of a sore throat and it gets rid of it straight away, and tastes lovely. I also use honey as an alternative to sugar on some of the cereals I like.

They're also mentioned in the bible, when God spoke to Moses in the burning bush, regarding the deliverance of Israel, from the Egyptians, and the place where He would lead them to.

Exodus 3:8 So I have come down to rescue them from the hand of the Egyptians, and to bring them up out of that land into a good and spacious land, a land flowing with **milk and honey.**

God indicates from this verse that these substances are good but also symbols of abundance. These would be found in the promised land and were luxuries. So, although these foods have countless nutritional properties for us, they are meant to be taken in moderation and not to excess.

> Milk and honey are good but are symbols of abundance and so should be used in moderation.

56

There are many benefits to milk; it's easy for us to break down; babies begin their lives with milk and it's a natural substance made by animals for animals. Nutritionally, it's one of the most complete and basic drinks we have. It's made up of calcium which is excellent for our bones and teeth and so helps to prevent osteoporosis. Potassium reduces the formation of kidney stones and helps to reduce blood pressure and the choline in it helps our sleep, learning and memory.[6]

I will reiterate the word of moderation again, though here, as too much milk could cause us to bulk up, as it contains saturated fat. Milk with lower fat contents are available though, and these still provide the benefits mentioned above. If you're lactose intolerant please stay away from milk too, unless you know you're divinely healed from it.

As I've said earlier, honey makes a great alternative to sugar and here we have a scripture that speaks of its goodness:

Proverbs 24:13 **Eat honey**, my son, for it is good; honey from the comb is sweet to your taste.

It's actually even better than just a natural sweetener, as it contains flavonoids and anti-oxidants that help prevent cancer and heart disease, it's anti-bacterial and helps to maintain constant energy levels and improves recovery times.[7] And as I've testified it also helps prevent sore throats.

---

[6] https://www.medicalnewstoday.com/articles/273451.php 04/10/2017 10:06

[7] http://www.realfoodforlife.com/health-benefits-of-honey/ 04/10/2017 15:37

Again, though we need to be careful how much we have:

Proverbs 25:16 If you find honey, **eat just enough** – too much of it, and you will vomit.

Water

Water is another obvious choice of drink. Water is essential for life. It is cleansing. When I did a search for water on the web there were 4,460,000,000[8] entries for it and in the King James translation of the bible, water is mentioned in 363 verses! About two thirds of our bodies is water, and over two thirds of the planet is water. For all that

> Water is the easiest liquid to digest and has no calories!

though, it remains one of the simplest compounds of any element and so is the easiest thing to digest and has no calories either!

In Judges 15, we read of the story of Samson when he killed the Philistines with the jawbone of an ass After he had done this he threw the jaw bone away and:

Judges 15:18-19 Because he was very thirsty, he cried out to the Lord, "You have given your servant this great victory. Must I now die of thirst and fall into the hands of the uncircumcised?" Then God opened up the hollow place in Lehi, and water came out of it. When Samson drank, his **strength** returned and he **revived**.

---

[8] As of 07/09/2017 15:08

This scripture shows us our need of water, God's provision and the benefits we can receive from it; our strength returning and being revived. Without enough hydration, our bodies can feel tired, as our blood thickens making it more difficult to pump through the body and transport nutrients and oxygen. So, without it, we could experience headaches, our skin could become dull and droopy and we could feel dizzy, confused, weak and light headed. Mood swings and irritability are also symptoms.[9] Water is needed for digestion, nutrient absorption, regulating circulation and body temperature, cushioning and lubricating joints, healthy skin and removal of waste products.

> Without enough water, our bodies can feel tired, as our blood thickens making it more difficult to pump though the body.

A few years ago, I had a large, ugly spot on my nose, it could've been a wart, I'm not sure, as I didn't go to the doctor to check. Nobody else noticed it, but it really brought me down and I hated it. I was just about to make an appointment to go the doctor to get it removed, when I realised I knew the Physician. The Physician, Who doesn't need to practise, but Who heals completely, without side effects. So, I laid my hands on the spot, spoke to it, in the name of Jesus, and told it to go. Nothing happened, I didn't see it disappear in front of my eyes. It was

---

[9] http://food.ndtv.com/health/headaches-mood-swings-fatigue-what-happens-when-you-dont-drink-enough-water-748882 07/09/2017 15:38

still there when I woke up the next day, **but** that same day I had the desire to just drink boiling water, (that had been cooled of course!) After two weeks of drinking boiled water, the spot/wart disappeared! I believe that was God's healing, not just a miracle that happened once, but a healing that has carried on for years. I still have a mug of boiled water most mornings since then, and have never had any more problems with my skin. Praise God.

> Make water your first and last drinks of the day.

The human body is about 60-70% water and we lose about 2.5 litres a day, so that's how much we need to absorb, to maintain our health. If we can drink about 1.8 litres a day, the rest we absorb when we eat. Good suggestions to make sure we get this fluid; is to make water our first and last drinks of the day – as we lose a lot of moisture at night. Maybe, keep a jug handy and carry a bottle of water around when going out. My mum used to wear bracelets and every time she had a drink, she would move one of them over to her other wrist so that she could see how many she had drunk, and that worked very well. The other point to remember is; when you're having

> Keep a jug of water handy throughout the day.

more drinks, you'll need to go to the toilet more as well! Don't put it off! Go! You'll be burning off calories just getting to the loo! Whilst I'm on the toilet subject, can I just add, be nice to your bowel! I think it's probably the only part of us that can't be trained! Have you heard of Irritable Bowel Syndrome? I believe it comes from – irritating your bowel! If it wants to go – let it! Whether it's in a public toilet, a friend's house or even church! Why do we get so anxious about it? We all do it, and if we don't let ourselves… well our bowels will let us know how irritated they are!

What to eat?

With regard to food, I believe I can eat "anything" I want, however I don't eat "everything." Look at this scripture:

1 Corinthians 6:12 "**Everything** is permissible for me" – but not everything is **beneficial**. "Everything is permissible for me" – but I will not be **mastered** by anything.

Here we can see that, yes, we can do (or in our case eat) everything we want, but not all things or foods are going to help us or be beneficial. We can have/eat everything we want, but some things could enslave

> We have to maintain a balance and we need to stay in control.

us if they're addictive (such as the sugar we've just mentioned). We have to maintain a balance and we need to stay in control. If you find there are certain products that you're addicted to, then the best way I've found to get over the addiction, is to go "cold turkey." It's difficult but effective. Such as, when I found myself having a chocolate milkshake, or three Mr Kipling apple pies a day, I stopped. I just didn't have them anymore. But, I didn't keep it up forever, only for as long as it took me to a) stop thinking about the certain food – so it's no longer a tradition or craving and b) get the weight off. But then I don't go back to the same old pattern either. Otherwise I'd end up in the same state as before.

Don't eat crisps. If I eat a bag of crisps every day for a week, I can tell by my belt that I have to stop! When I was pregnant, the professionals told me I wasn't big/heavy enough, so I'd eat crisps for a week and put weight on straight away!! How bad was that? Looking back, it was absolutely pathetic, because the weight gain wasn't the baby at all but the saturated fat! It's funny isn't it - the reasons we have for eating. We always have to be alert and use wisdom.

Don't fry food. There are other ways of cooking that are a lot healthier for us, such as baking and of course grilling. I don't own a deep fat fryer and have never owned a chip pan. I do have a frying pan, but it's normally used to make meals with sauces, such as Bolognese. If I have chips I use oven ones, they're easier to make, healthier and don't make the kitchen smell.

Don't have fast food. My husband, God bless him, introduced me to McDonald's breakfasts a while ago and I became addicted to them. It got to the point where I was willing to pay to eat one on my own! And, I've never done anything like that. It didn't take me long to realise I needed to do something about it and haven't had one since! Don't be afraid to give up things, we have so much else that we can have instead.

> Don't be afraid to give up foods, there's so many others we can have instead.

Olive Oil

A good fat to have in our diet is olive oil, as it has a lot of nutritional value. Not only to the inside of our bodies but also our skin, hair and nails as well!

According to the Olive Oil Times on the Internet, it can help prevent several cancers, as it's rich in natural anti-oxidants which prevent cell damage, diabetes type 2 and **depression**.[10]

In the bible, it's actually referred to as, 'the oil of joy' ('gladness' in the Amplified and KJV) and so it would seem that science is agreeing with God's wisdom at last!

> Science is agreeing with God's wisdom at last!

Psalm 45:7 You love righteousness and hate wickedness, therefore God, your God, has set you above your companions by anointing you with the **oil of joy**.

For the skin, it can be used to treat wounds, as it makes the skin suppler and elastic, and so heals better. In the story of the Good Samaritan, it was used to treat the man who was robbed:

Luke 10:34 He went to him and bandaged his wounds pouring on **oil** and wine.

Have a little look online and see what you think, also find out where you can add it to your own diet.

---

[10] https://www.oliveoiltimes.com/olive-oil-health-benefits/ 04/10/2017 0928

There are a lot of olive oils on the market but the best one to use, is Extra Virgin, as this is the least tampered with. It hasn't been heated, processed or had any extra chemicals added to it. But again, go online and see what you think as the information changes often.

How big are your portions?

How big are your portions? Can you decrease these without missing out on anything? A good trick is **not** to miss out on anything but just have everything in moderation. Maybe, just change your plate, having one that is smaller than the one before, then your eyes will think you're having just as much as normal. If you have decided to cut something out of your diet, (like fizzy pop) don't feel you're missing out on anything, concentrate on what you will gain from not having it instead. In

> If you cut something out, don't feel like you're missing out, concentrate on what you will gain.

general, though, I believe balance is good, a little of all the food groups in moderation. I know there are certain diets which avoid carbohydrates or proteins, but Jesus served five loaves and two fish, and He wouldn't have done that, if they were going to harm us.

Normally we eat what we don't like first, leaving the best for last, but I reckon, eat what you like first, and then if you get full, you won't mind leaving what's left over. You don't have to eat everything on your plate! I know people are starving around the

64

world, but it's not going to help them, or you, if you eat **every** mouthful, is it?

When are you eating?

Is it late at night? Try not to eat after six o'clock. It makes logical sense when you think about it: as the earlier you eat the longer you have, to burn the calories off. Eating just before going to bed, means you have very little time to burn the calories.

If you always get hungry after an early dinner just say, "No," to yourself, I guarantee you within a week – you'll stop getting hungry – I've done it myself. Don't forget our bodies are like children! Our flesh, if we let it, will do what it wants when it wants! But we're not just flesh. We're souls and spirits as well. Our souls/minds can control our flesh. We just have to say, "No," sometimes. Train our bodies like a child. Be firm; don't give in, no matter what! If our bodies start having a tantrum, ignore them!

> If our bodies start having a tantrum, ignore them!

Don't snack! What's the point? They don't fill us up. Yes, they're tasty but they're secretly sabotaging our plans to get healthy and slim. So, again train yourself to not want them.

A good tool to eating the right things, is to make a plan, whether it be a daily one or a weekly one, but make a plan of what to eat and when to eat it, and then stick to it.

65

What do I do?

Personally, I try to have three meals a day, and only very rarely snack. I enjoy the meals I have, they're always very tasty, filling and enjoyable, so then I don't need to snack because my taste buds are satisfied and my stomach is too! I have a routine, so my body knows exactly how much it's going to get in the day, and if it wants more, most of the time I will tell it, "No!"

I am convinced that one day you will be able to eat whatever you want – but NOT EVERY DAY – you will always have to say, "No," sometimes – otherwise your stomachs will become your masters again.

> One day you will be able to eat whatever you want – but not every day!

Going forward

So first of all, ask God what you need to give up. He knows you completely, He made you, He made you differently from everyone else, He can tell you what your key is. Then when the Lord tells you what to do, do it!

In the meantime, stay away from sugar and fried food, eat and drink things that haven't been messed around with, such as water, fruit and vegetables. Have a think about how much you're eating and when you're eating it.

Try, also not to let this become the main focus of your life. Don't exchange food and eating being gods, to diets and slimming being gods instead! We need to keep our thoughts and minds on our Lord Jesus at all times. Let's change our lifestyles, but keep our hearts and minds stayed on Him.

5. BASIC ESSENTIALS

In this chapter, we're going to talk about the basic essentials that the Lord has given us to live fully. God has provided these things for our benefit and the best thing of all, is that they're FREE OF CHARGE! I've already talked about water in the last chapter, so I won't cover it again, instead here are some others that, I believe, will prove to be essential.

Sleep

Amazingly, lack of sleep can be a contributory factor in obesity. According to livestrong.com a person of 150 pounds (10 stone 10 pounds in the UK) will burn off 500 calories during an eight-hour sleep.[11] This is because when we're asleep, hormones and chemicals that control appetite are released, so when we get enough, we don't get so hungry during the day. Lack of sleep can also cause a lot of other problems as well, I'm sure we all agree that it's dangerous to drive when tired, but it can also affect our health; physically and mentally too.

> When we get enough sleep, we don't get so hungry during the day!

Hence, it's extremely important to sleep and thankfully we have promises in the bible that we can stand on, to be able to get it:

Psalm 127:2 (last part) For He grants **sleep to those He loves**.

---

[11] http://www.livestrong.com/article/434236-why-do-you-lose-weight-after-a-nights-sleep/ 15/09/2017 14:25

Psalm 4:8 I will lie down and **sleep in peace**, for You alone, O Lord, make me dwell in safety.

Remember, we **are loved** by the Lord, we know this because He sent Jesus to die for us (John 3:16 For God **so loved** the world that He gave His one and only Son) – He can't love us any more than that – so He will 'grant us sleep.' We'll be safe as we sleep too, as the Lord protects us. We don't have to fret – even if we're alone and it's dark!

Why is it difficult then?

Why do many people (including Christians) have problems falling asleep? Is it because we worry? I know my mind can wander a lot at times. We need to try and fix our thoughts on the Lord as much as possible. Fix them on His Word and promises and then it will be easier for us to relax. Don't worry! It is possible! The Lord commanded us not to worry! And it would be unfair of Him to say it, if it was impossible.

Luke 12:22 and 31 Then Jesus said to his disciples: "Therefore I tell you, **do not worry** about your life, what you will eat; or about your body, what you will wear." "But seek His kingdom, and these things will be given to you as well."

Another wonderful verse to help us not to worry is from Proverbs 3:5-6 **Trust in the Lord** with all your heart and lean not on your own understanding; in all your ways acknowledge Him, and He will make your paths straight.

These were my favourite passages of scripture for a long time, as I used to worry about anything I could at one point. However, by meditating on these verses (for a long time) I realised that worrying didn't solve anything and learnt that, by fixing my eyes on Jesus; remembering His power, ability and love; the things I used to worry about, fixed themselves a lot easier. I can't seriously remember when I last worried now – really! Because I know, really know, that the Lord will sort everything out for me – as He has done in the past and will continue to do so now and in the future. It was only the other week when I had a dilemma, I needed to be in two places at the same time – helping people out as you do – but even before I remembered to ask the Lord to help, He had already sorted it out and given me two solutions! He really is great, going before us and after us, making our paths straight and giving us peace. Instead of worrying then, I recommend meditating on His Word. Maybe use those two scriptures I've given (about sleeping) from Psalms, just think on them over and over again. Ponder on the verses the same way you agonised over your problems. Think them all the way through, upside down and back to front. Take every single word and think of what it means. I'm sure it will be easier to get to sleep then.

> Fixing my eyes on Jesus; remembering His power, ability and love; the things I used to worry about, fixed themselves a lot easier.

> Instead of worrying, meditate on His Word. Ponder on the verses the same way we agonised over our problems.

70

How did Daniel sleep?

A great example in the bible of someone being able to sleep, instead of worrying, knowing the Lord's love, provision, power and ability is Daniel. Chapter 2 of Daniel is one of the stories about King Nebuchadnezzar. Nebuchadnezzar had had a lot of dreams and wanted to know the interpretation of them. So, he got all the magicians, astrologers and sorcerers in the land together, along with Daniel, and told them if they didn't tell him what the dreams meant, he would kill them. The huge problem was – he couldn't remember them! Daniel – instead of panicking - simply asked for some time to do this and here we pick up the story:

Daniel 2:17-19 Then Daniel went to his house, and made the thing known to Hananiah, Mishael, and Azariah, his companions: That they would desire mercies of the God of heaven concerning this secret; that Daniel and his fellows should not perish with the rest of the wise men of Babylon. Then was the secret revealed unto Daniel in a **night** vision. (KJV)

What's a night vision? A dream! So that means, Daniel must have fallen asleep! Even though he knew his life was on the line, he slept! That really is knowing the Lord's peace. How did he do it, because he went to the Lord, he gave his problem to Him, and had the faith, that the Lord would reveal the answer. And the Lord did.

71

In the Old and New Testaments alike, we're told to give our problems to the Lord:

Psalm 55:22 **Cast your cares** on the Lord and He will sustain you; He will never let the righteous fall.

1 Peter 5:7 **Cast all your anxiety** on Him because He cares for you.

Let's not hold onto our problems or cares, instead let's sleep peacefully knowing the Lord cares for us and that He will never let us down.

Isaiah 26:3 You will keep in **perfect peace** him whose mind is steadfast, because he trusts in You.

Wow, that's exactly what we need to get a good night's sleep!

More tips to get some sleep

Here are a few practical approaches that may also help:

- Go to bed and wake up at regular times – even on weekends.
- Have a regular bedtime routine – begin an hour before we expect to fall asleep.
- Make sure our bedrooms are dark, quiet, comfortable and cool.
- Use the bedroom for sleeping only – no televisions, computers or books.

- Finish eating 2-3 hours before going to bed.
- Exercise regularly during the day.
- Avoid caffeine and alcohol close to bedtime.
- Make sleep a priority, don't just go to bed once everything else is done.
- Have a notebook by our beds, so if something (or many things) are on our minds we can write them down and think about them the following day.

Personally, I found that reading would keep me awake, as it would stimulate me too much. So, I avoid that. I know it doesn't happen to everyone, but you could be one of those people like me! Reading the bible however, doesn't give me the same problem, probably due to the verse mentioned earlier, regarding our minds being stayed upon the Lord. Also having a bath increased my heart rate – I probably had it too hot – so I either have a morning shower or have a bath early in the evening, to give myself a couple of hours to cool down instead.

We shouldn't pressurise ourselves to fall asleep either. One night I couldn't get to sleep because I knew I had an early morning and needed the sleep more than normal. But could I drop off? No, instead the more I demanded myself to sleep, the less I felt like it! In the end, I gave up making myself go to sleep and just told myself to rest, then within a few minutes I dropped off! Unfortunately, a human characteristic is to always do the opposite of what is being commanded. By commanding myself to sleep, my body went into rebellion! So, my advice is, when you go to bed; go to rest, enjoy the

> The more I demanded myself to sleep, the less I felt like it!

peace, enjoy the relaxation, and don't make it a big deal actually nodding off!

Anger:

Hmm, so now, what about anger? It's definitely difficult to relax when we're angry, with all the emotions and thoughts racing around in our heads! Although some anger is Godly - Jesus was angry with the merchants in the temple (John 2:12-17), Moses threw the tablets of the law down (Exodus 32:19) - a lot of it needs to be dealt with as soon as possible, and if we can we should do that:

Ephesians 4:26 ... do not let the sun go down while you are still **angry**.

However, a lot of the time we won't be able to sort out the problem with the person whom we're angry with straight away, so we'll need to give it to the Lord instead. When I'm filled with anger, I think of what the Lord endured on the cross to take away my sins – the same punishment He endured for everyone's sins.

> When I'm angry I think of what the Lord endured on the cross to take away my sins and everyone else's.

That punishment was way beyond the punishment I would want to inflict on anyone – no matter what they've done to me, and so it quells my anger too.

Ephesians 4:32 Be kind and compassionate to one another, **forgiving each other**, just as in Christ God forgave you.

74

So, we should give our hurts and offences away, the person that has offended us may not even know we're angry with them anyway, we're only hurting ourselves by keeping the offence. We need to give these problems to Jesus, remember His punishment and let them go, at least until we can do something about them, and talk to the person. Don't let them rob us of our sleep and rest. Let's face it, a lack of sleep makes us feel irritable, so the problem could get worse, whereas after a good night's rest, maybe everything will seem better anyway.

Too much sleep:

At this point, I probably should point out that too much sleep can also cause problems as well.

Proverbs 19:15 **Laziness** brings on deep sleep, and the shiftless man goes hungry.

Proverbs 20:13 Do not love sleep or you will grow **poor**.

If we're sleeping all the time, we may be burning off calories, but we're not getting anything done!

If we're sleeping all the time, we may not be eating, we may be burning off calories but we're not getting anything done! We're not living, we're not working, or enjoying the time, body and abilities the Lord has given us. So, there's a balance we must find. Maybe it would be best to set a target of between 7-9 hours a night, no less than 6 and no more than 10, to get the most out of sleep but not let it control us, by having too much.

Laughter

According to the BBC website, laughing just 15-20 minutes a day can burn off 5lbs a year![12] As our heart beats faster, we use muscles and burn calories. What a wonderful way to lose weight! So, are you too serious? Do you need to laugh more? Put on a funny DVD tonight and have a good laugh, laugh with your children, laugh with the neighbours, never miss an opportunity to giggle! My nan laughs all the time, and she has lived to a good old age, even though her main diet is fried food! She's never had a problem with weight either, so maybe this is her secret!

> Laughing 15-20 minutes a day can burn off 5lbs a year!

Proverbs 17:22 A **cheerful** heart is good medicine: but a crushed spirit dries up the bones.

The Lord gave us a sense of humour. We were made to laugh, to have joy. I always feel so much better after a good laugh. It breaks the tension and just makes me feel great. It's wonderful there are now so many proven health benefits to laughter as well: Here are some of them; laughter helps prevent heart disease, as it increases the blood flow and improves the function of blood vessels. It reduces stress, anxiety and fear, improves moods and releases endorphins. Laughter can also strengthen relationships, improve teamwork and help resolve conflict.[13]

---

[12] http://news.bbc.co.uk/1/hi/health/6274119.stm 06/10/2017 10:55
[13] https://en.wikipedia.org/wiki/Laughter 15/09/2017 13:33

There are a couple of well known, although rather unorthodox medical centres which use humour and laughter as therapies. Dr Francisco Contreras of the Oasis of Hope clinic in Mexico says, "Positive emotions invoked by humour have healing effects," and "Joy is vital to the recuperation of health. One bout of anger will diminish the efficiency of your immune system for six hours, but one good laugh will **increase** the efficiency of your immune system for twenty-four hours."[14] and considering the clinic, of which he is director, president and chairman of, has treated over 100,000 patients with cancer since 1963, I think he knows what he's saying. Have you ever watched the film Patch Adams? Well, it's loosely based on a real doctor called Hunter Doherty "Patch" Adams who desired to be compassionately connected with his patients and used humour and play to help their cure.[15] According to them, they've had great success with their therapies, and as they're in line with scripture, I believe them.

> "One good laugh will increase the efficiency of your immune system for twenty-four hours!"

So, let's put on a funny film, have a night with our mates, talk to our children and have a good laugh – humour can be found in so many places - I mean the way our digestive systems work at times! Wind! The noise, the smell! Of course, we do have to be careful who we are sharing that with, but it always makes me laugh! I think, the Lord really has got a good sense of humour inventing that for us!

---

[14] http://www.positivitylife.com/humor-is-healing/ 15/09/2017 13:44
[15] https://en.wikipedia.org/wiki/Patch_Adams 15/09/2017 14:02

What makes us depressed anyway?

Romans 8:28 And we know that in all things God works for the **good** of those who love Him, who have been called according to His purpose.

Psalm 37:13 But the Lord **laughs** at the wicked for He knows their day is coming.

Now the second of these two scriptures, is obviously from the Old Testament, and the wicked are now saved by grace, should they choose to receive it, as much as we are. But the principle is the same. God is on our side. God is always working for our good. We are winners, no matter what comes our way, whatever happens to us, we are conquerors, and we should be able to laugh like the Lord does, because we know at the end of the day: we will win.

Romans 8:37 No, in all these things **we are more than conquerors** through Him Who loved us.

Again, how can we be depressed? If all else fails and we die, we go to be with the Lord – that's great news! We'll be in heaven where there is fullness and wholeness and wonder! But the Lord loves us now too. The maker of heaven and earth loves us and wants intimate relationships with us now. Who cares what our neighbours think of us? Who cares if our spouses have a go at us or even leave us? The King over the whole earth loves us, just the way we are!

Isaiah 54:5 For your **Maker is your Husband** – the Lord Almighty is His name – the Holy One of Israel is your Redeemer; He is called the God of all the earth.

When, my first husband left me, this was the verse God gave me. And, this turned my depression into joy! It can do the same for you because surely, out of all the people in the world we have more to laugh about, than any. We are **in** the Light, we **are** the light, so surely, we can **be** light hearted. There's no need for us to fear anything; not people, not problems, not even death!

> We are **in** the light, we **are** the light, so surely, we can **be** light hearted.

Sunshine

Psalm 84:11 For the Lord God is a **sun** and shield, the Lord bestows favour and honour, no good thing does He withhold from those whose walk is blameless.

Ecclesiastes 7:11 Wisdom, like an inheritance is a good thing and benefits those who see the **sun**.

There's a lot of interest surrounding the effects of sunshine and particularly vitamin D (that we get from the sun) around at the moment. Vitamin D is essential to healthy living. So, the Lord really knew what He was doing, when He created it!

Vitamin D can also be found in certain foods such as dairy products, egg yolks and fatty fish, so if you don't get to see the sun very much, these are the foods to eat, but the easiest and fastest way to absorb the vitamin, is still sunlight.

What does this wonderful vitamin do for us? It doesn't actually lose any weight for us, but it possibly could help the reasons why we're eating in the first place and it's also amazing for our bodies and general health. It helps us absorb calcium and phosphate which of course are important for healthy bones, teeth and muscles. It helps to prevent osteoporosis and rickets in children, which are both bone diseases. Not only that, but there's evidence to suggest it also helps to prevent diabetes type 1 and multiple sclerosis.[16] [17]

Seasonal affective disorder – SAD – is a form of depression that occurs in relation to the seasons, most commonly beginning in winter, when the days become shorter and there's less sunlight. It occurs because our bodies crave the sun and the symptoms **may include weight gain, from craving carbohydrates to compensate**.[18]

So, let's get outdoors and into the sunshine. Thankfully we should be able to get all of our vitamin D in the summer months when the days are longer, and there's more chance of sunny weather. Spend time doing the gardening, going for a walk or just sitting outside and reading a book.

---

[16] http://www.nhs.uk/Livewell/Summerhealth/Pages/vitamin-D-sunlight.aspx 17/09/2017 11:30

[17] https://www.medicalnewstoday.com/articles/161618.php 17/09/2017 11:37

[18] http://www.nhs.uk/conditions/seasonal-affective-disorder/pages/introduction.aspx 17/09/2017 12:17

Now at this point, I must remind us all to be wise, too much sunlight can lead to sunburn! Which isn't nice at all – I'm afraid I've suffered from this far too often and don't even need to research the effects on the websites! We need to be careful and use sun cream, making sure we apply it before our skin turns red. We also need to drink plenty of water.

But as you can see from the scriptures, I used before, the Lord made the sun to be good – He called it "Good" when He made it on the fourth day of creation (Genesis 1:17-19). He has made it to be beneficial to all of us. It's free! So, let's enjoy it; with wisdom and not with fear.

Fellowship

When God created man, He didn't make us to live alone. That's why the Lord made Eve - it wasn't good for Adam (the perfect man, made in the direct image of God) to be on his own. If it wasn't good for him; it's not good for us, so we need to spend time with one another.

> Sharing problems and issues may not halve them, but could actually solve them!

There is a profound dynamic in fellowship. Sharing problems and sharing issues may not halve them, but can actually solve them. Just being with someone else – especially in the faith – can help us work out problems and come to solutions. I have a lot of friends; Christian, saved-but-not-practising-Christian and definitely-not Christian at all! I love them all though and think they love me back. When I'm with them, the conversations can go anywhere – no topics

81

are taboo and they're really fun and uplifting. There have been many times when their advice and guidance has really helped me make important decisions and their support has encouraged me to keep going too.

We don't get so depressed if we spend time with friends. I know relationships have definitely helped me through some rough times. Talking therapies are recommended to people with

> **What do we do with friends? Talk! Laugh!**

depression,[19] and what do you do with a mate? Talk. Not only talk, but chat and laugh and have fun! I always feel so much better after spending time with someone else. I feel elated, happy, ecstatic even.

I'm sure fellowship helps slimming too. Being with other people who can encourage us, who can tell us the truth, who can laugh with us and remind us how lovely we are, will motivate us to keep going and not quit. (Obviously if you have friends, that are in the same situation as you and of the same mindset – it will be of greater advantage, because you can really help one another by understanding what the other is going through.)

My family have always been on my side, they're wonderful and I know I'm lucky to have them. So that's a good place to start (when looking for friends) then there are churches, gyms, social clubs and lots of other places to meet people. Find someone that will be on your side, that will support you and love you, and then spend time with them, support and love them back!

---

[19] http://www.nhs.uk/Conditions/stress-anxiety-depression/Pages/benefits-of-talking-therapy.aspx 18/09/2017 13:48

Hebrews 10:25 Let us not give up **meeting together** …. but let us **encourage one another**….

I'm persuaded this is not solely talking about going to church, but also getting together with other Christians, so that we can talk over problems and concerns that are important to us as individuals. Get together with the knowledge that, "For where two or three come together in My Name, there am I with them." (Matthew 18:20) And wow, when the Lord is with us, He brings a whole new dimension.

Ecclesiastes 4:9-12 **Two are better than one**, because they have a good return for their work: If one falls down, his friend can help him up. But pity the man who falls and has no-one to help him up! Also, if two lie down together, they will keep warm. But how can one keep warm alone? Though one may be overpowered, two can defend themselves. A cord of **three strands** is not quickly broken.

We can see clearly from this passage that fellowship has many benefits. And the third strand mentioned in the cord, is Jesus, Who heals us, delivers us and reveals to us His solutions. Whatever our needs, He can bring them to pass. With a friend and Jesus, we can be invincible!

> With a friend and Jesus, we can be invincible!

A quick warning though, be choosy when picking friends. Love everyone, but choose your company wisely. Choose friends that are positive, encouraging, that build you up and make sure, in return, you are being as positive and encouraging back.

83

1 Corinthians 15:33 Do not be misled, "**Bad company corrupts good character.**"

Psalm 1:1 Blessed is the man who **does not** walk in the counsel of the wicked, or stand in the way of sinners, or sit in the seat of mockers.

Being with friends that want to eat all the time, are very negative on life, or who are angry all the time can have a negative impact on us instead, as these verses suggest. So, we need to be picky and choose, with care, who we spend time with.

There was a long period of my life when I didn't have any friends. I was blessed enough to have my husband and family, but no friends. I didn't have time for friends, all my time was spent working. I had never gone to school where I lived and worked alone, so there didn't seem to be any opportunities to make friends. The church I went to didn't do much socialising either. So, I asked the Lord for help (always takes me a while) but shortly after He gave me the opportunity to help at a Christian conference and since then I've made wonderful friends who have stood the test of time and tricky situations! I also had a son, who was a wonderful excuse to join mother and baby groups and gave me common ground with other women and mums. I've found since then, it's actually easy to make friends! There are more lonely people out there than you'd think.

Relationships take work as well:

Proverbs 18:24 A man who has friends must himself be **friendly**.

We need to make time for relationships too. We need to make an effort to stay in contact with friends, and spend time together, but what a blessing when we do! Yes, there will be times when they let us down, but we may let them down as well (possibly!) But the advantages far outweigh the disadvantages, so give them a go!

Singing

People have always sung. There are numerous references to singing in the bible and as practising Christians we're encouraged to sing praise to the Lord always.

Psalm 34:1 I will **extol** the Lord at all times; His **praise** will always be on my lips.

Philippians 4:4 **Rejoice** in the Lord always. I will say it again: **Rejoice!**

But did you know that, singing is actually good for us as well? It's an aerobic activity which is good for our hearts and lungs.[20] It exercises the upper muscles in our bodies and can be done when sitting down! It releases endorphins (the same chemicals that are released when we eat a chocolate bar) so that we feel better and it reduces cortisol (a chemical that is released when we're stressed to calm us down) so that we don't feel so anxious.[21] This means that, singing may stop us from eating so

---

[20] https://heartresearch.org.uk/fundraising/singing-good-you 17/09/2017 15:40

[21] http://ideas.time.com/2013/08/16/singing-changes-your-brain/ 17/09/2017 15:42

much chocolate! So, although it doesn't directly help us lose weight, I believe it will definitely help us, indirectly. Group singing is even better! Because we're in fellowship as well. What do we do in church? Group singing! If we want to make friendships and sing, and don't like church (or don't have a decent one nearby to go to) why not join a choir. It would really benefit us in a lot of ways and help us to lose the weight we want.

> Everything the Lord asks us to do for Him, benefits **us!**

The Lord never ceases to amaze me either. Everything He has created is good. Everything He asks us to do, to bless Him, **benefits us** at the same time! There is no other god like Him, He is fantastic.

Psalm 147:1 Praise the Lord. How **good** it is to **sing praises** to our God, how pleasant and fitting to praise Him.

In fact, I would encourage you to read all of Psalm 147 as it gives us so many reasons to praise His Name.

Going forward

Plan to sleep more, get out in the sunshine, spend more time with friends (or make some) laugh and sing!

The Lord really has provided us with so many good things, that are free, that are available to all of us. We just need to use them, and make the most of them.

6. FASTING

I did a quick test on Google to see how many articles there were on 'why we should fast,' and it came up with over 2 billion. I did another search to find out how many articles there were to say, 'why we shouldn't fast," and it came up with 71 million.[22] So, there are a lot of contrasting views out there, but it does have the majority. I would also like to ask, "Would the Lord ask us to do anything that was bad for us?" No! "Is the Lord completely good?" Yes! Well, in that case as it was the Lord that first instigated fasting in the Old Testament in the days of Moses, I think we should give it a go. There were fasts for different holy days such as the Day of Atonement, and Jesus encouraged us to continue fasting once He returned to the Father...

Matthew 9:15 Jesus answered, "How can the guests of the Bridegroom mourn while He is with them? The time will come when the Bridegroom will be taken from them; then **they will fast**.

So, contrary to what it says in most diet books, I'm going to suggest fasting, as of course ultimately it will help us to lose weight as well. Less calories in, more pounds off.

Less calories in = more pounds off

Both the Oxford Dictionary and the Strong's definition of fasting is to abstain from food. I've heard it taught that we can fast from anything that can take us away from spending time with the

---

[22] Searches carried out on 18/09/2017 14:45

Lord, such as watching television, which is great, but here we're going to focus on the technical term of fasting, not eating.

Physical benefits

It's medically beneficial to fast: Instead of our bodies working hard to digest a steady supply of food, they can get to work clearing the many toxins that have built up in our bodies during our lives instead. Fasting helps our bodies to detox and repair cells, tissues and organs.

During our normal routine, our digestive systems are always on the go, whilst during a fast they get a much-needed rest.

Here are some of the other ailments it can help to fight: arthritis, as it clears all the joints around the body, stomach upsets and bowel problems, skin conditions, cardio vascular disease, asthma and diabetes type 1.[23]   It doesn't cure any of these, but it does give our bodies the chance to heal themselves,[24] which they were programmed to do by our Creator.

Spiritual benefits

Not only this, but fasting has spiritual benefits too. First of course, it's intended to take our minds off food and onto God

---

[23] http://www.activebeat.co/diet-nutrition/8-things-you-need-to-know-about-fasting 18/09/2017 15:00

[24] http://www.allaboutfasting.com/benefits-of-fasting.html 18/09/2017 15:14

(Who should take our first thought anyway) and second, belief comes from prayer and fasting; or rather unbelief goes with prayer and fasting. Here's one of the stories about Jesus, from Matthew to prove it.

> **Unbelief goes with prayer and fasting.**

Matthew 17:14–21 And when they had come to the multitude, a man came to Him, kneeling down to Him and saying, "Lord, have mercy on my son, for he is an epileptic and suffers severely; for he often falls into the fire and often into the water. So I brought him to Your disciples, but they could not cure him." Then Jesus answered and said, "O faithless and perverse generation, how long shall I be with you? How long shall I bear with you? Bring him here to Me." And Jesus rebuked the demon, and it came out of him; and the child was cured from that very hour. Then the disciples came to Jesus privately and said, "Why could we not cast it out?" So Jesus said to them, "**Because of your unbelief**; for assuredly, I say to you, if you have faith as a mustard seed, you will say to this mountain, 'Move from here to there,' and it will move; and nothing will be impossible for you. However, **this kind** does not go out except by prayer and fasting." (NKJV)

I have put in bold the point I am trying to make: the 'this kind" does not refer to the type of devil, but instead to the unbelief, (also in bold) that Jesus was speaking about in the previous

89

verse. Fasting gets rid of unbelief. Or rather, prayer and fasting gets rid of unbelief. It's the combination of the two that gives profound results. It certainly makes more sense. If we try and rebuke devils because of what **we** have done (in this case fasting) they would probably laugh at us. Who are we anyway? It's at the Name of Jesus that every knee shall bow (Philippians 2:10). But you see during a fast, we concentrate on the Lord, and focus on what **He** has done for us, who **He** is and then **He's** where we get the power.

> During a fast we concentrate on what **He** has done of us, who **He** is and that **He's** where we get the power to cast out devils.

Fasting, also gives us a sense of urgency for whatever we need, instead of being willing to compromise, instead of looking to society or our own intellect to help, we rely on supernatural power, the power of Jesus, to resolve our issue. So, what are you believing for at the moment? Could you do with getting rid of some of your unbelief? Do you need some supernatural power in your life? Maybe fasting could be your answer.

More reasons to fast

In the Old Testament, during the time of the law and the Ten Commandments, fasting was a command and a way of getting the Lord on the Israelites side. Since Jesus came and fulfilled the law, fasting no longer moves God, nor does it make Him love us anymore. Fasting, however still has benefits for us as it takes away unbelief as mentioned above and helps us to seek (and hear) the Lord's direction and guidance:

Acts 13:3 So after they had **fasted** and prayed, they placed their hands on them and sent them off.

Acts 14:23 Paul and Barnabas appointed elders for them in each church and, with prayer and **fasting**, committed them to the Lord, in Whom they had put their trust.

If we deliberately decide to go on a fast, and stick to it, then we are in fact controlling our bodies, rather than letting our bodies control us, this in turn allows our spirits to be a more dominant force in our lives. Once our spirits have more control over our thoughts and desires, they will have more of an impact on more areas than just food. We'll be able to hear the Lord more clearly and, in time, we may be able to control our bodies so that we can accept healing, deliverance and prosperity with more ease than we do now. You see, feelings and the truth have very little in common. Although we may "feel" hungry during a fast, we can be sure that:

Matthew 4:4 Jesus answered, "It is written, 'Man does not live on bread alone, but on every Word that comes from the mouth of God,'"

John 6:35 Then Jesus declared, "I am the bread of life. He who comes to me will never go hungry, and he who believes in me will never be thirsty"

The truth is, the Lord is our portion. (Psalm 119:57) He's the One Who sustains us. If we can understand and have a revelation over this, then food can no longer have a hold on us. Then if we need the Lord's power in other areas of our lives, we can find the truths in the bible for those too, and instead of relying on our feelings to tell us what or who we are, we can find out what the Word says. For instance, we may feel sick, but the truth in His Word says: "By His wounds you have been healed" 1 Peter 2:24 Or when we feel depressed, His Word says: "You fill me with joy in Your presence." (Psalm 16:11)

How to fast - 1

So, what happens when we start to fast? Well, our bodies will rebel. That's a fact! They won't like it! They won't like it at all! But always remember they will get to eat again!

> When we fast, our bodies won't like it, they won't like it at all! But they will eat again!

So, the first tip is, to decide in our hearts that we're going to have a fast.

2 Corinthians 9:7 Each man should give what he has **decided in his heart** to give, not reluctantly or under compulsion, for God loves a cheerful giver.

This refers to offerings; however, I believe we can use the same principle when we fast. It isn't nice giving money away, when we need it to pay bills and buy food, so we have to decide in our

92

hearts what to give, and then the Lord supernaturally meets our needs in return. Likewise, it's not nice to go without meals, so, we need to decide in our hearts to fast too. We need to be sure that we want to fast and then do it cheerfully. If we haven't got it set in our minds it will be too easy to give up. The length of time you fast for, is entirely up to you and the Lord, it could be two meals, it could be two weeks. Please, note here, if we don't do it, don't beat ourselves up about it. The Lord loves us still! He is the answer, not our works, and any amount of time will help the slimming anyway.

Be prepared. Being forewarned is like being forearmed. It's difficult to fast. Here are some of the symptoms that may occur; fatigue, aches, pains, irritability and headaches. These are caused by the toxins being eliminated from our blood. So, rest. This will make the fast more productive anyway, as the calories we need to burn off will come from our fat rather than muscle.[25] I once did a Zumba class after fasting for the day, and wondered why I felt faint!! It didn't take me long to work it out thankfully, but please learn from my mistake rather than making it yourself.

> **Don't forget to drink more water than normal.**

Don't forget to drink plenty of water too, more than normal, as we get a lot of hydration from the food we eat. The body needs water to survive – and although we can go without food for a certain length of time we can't go without water – without causing serious problems.

---

[25] http://www.activebeat.co/diet-nutrition/8-things-you-need-to-know-about-fasting/3/ 22/09/2017 15:27

If you go on a long fast, the first three days are the worst but then the symptoms do get better. Don't fast if you are under the age of eighteen, pregnant, diabetic or recovering from an operation, as your systems are dealing with a lot of other things already.[26]

How to fast – 2

Another thing to consider during a fast is our attitude, the Lord Himself mentioned it in the gospels.

Matthew 6:16-18 "When you fast, **do not look sombre** as the hypocrites do, for they disfigure their faces to show men they are fasting. I tell you the truth, they have received their reward in full. But when you fast, put oil on your head and wash your face, so that it will not be obvious to men that you are fasting, but only to your Father, who is unseen; and your Father, who sees what is done in secret will reward you," (openly. KJV ending)

So, keep your heads up, remember you **will** have food again – don't let your bodies deceive you – you won't starve! There **is** food in the cupboard, there **is** food in the shop! There **is** food everywhere! We are **not** in a war situation. We need to keep positive, so don't resent watching other people eat either, instead be happy for them.

> Don't let your bodies deceive you – you won't starve!

---

[26] http://www.activebeat.co/diet-nutrition/8-things-you-need-to-know-about-fasting/7 25/09/2017 14:21

Isaiah 58:7 Is it not (talking about fasting) to share your food with the hungry and to provide the poor wanderer with shelter – when you see the naked, to clothe him, and not to turn away from your own flesh and blood? (Brackets mine)

Here it's saying that on a fast, the point is to actually give your food to someone else who needs it. Maybe if you're working in town, you could still make your lunch, but give it to someone who is homeless instead. Give out of love, fast out of love, do not fast out of a guilty conscience, or out of a need to make God work for you. Fast because you want to, because you realise that it will benefit you. Sometimes I dream of going on a retreat, being alone with books, films and of course the Lord for company. It would be somewhere beautiful with long walks over hills and valleys so I could appreciate the Lord's majesty and handiwork. I wouldn't cook, or wash up – I would fast; sounds amazing don't you agree? I wonder what my faith would be like after that?

> Fast out of love, because it will benefit you.

Isaiah 58:6 & 8 "Is not this the kind of fasting I have chosen: to loose the chains of injustice and untie the cords of the yoke, to set the oppressed free and break every yoke? Then your light will break forth like the dawn, and **your healing will quickly appear**; then your righteousness will go before you, and the glory of the Lord will be your rear guard.

Wow! Fasting is certainly worth our time and energy!

How to finish a fast

If we fast for four days or more at a time, we also need to be careful how we start eating normally again. It needs to be done over a couple of days or longer, as eating too much can have bad results, such as stomach cramping, nausea and vomiting.[27] We should also start on something small and easy to digest. Don't have a steak or something that takes a lot for the body to break up, instead maybe have fruit, vegetables or small dairy products like yogurts.

So, what do I do? Well for most of my adult life I have fasted two meals a week – on the same day – I fast my breakfast and lunch, only eating my main meal in the evening. I drink only water (the occasional hot chocolate) and coffee during it. I do it as regularly as I can. I believe it has helped me to maintain my weight and my faith in the Lord. It isn't a religion because if I forget or fail, I remember that I'm saved by grace and not works. If I have a break from it, it does feel harder to re-start, so doing it each week is easier in the long run.

Going forward

If you're excited by the benefits of fasting and want to give it a go, the first thing to do is decide when you're going to do it and for how long. If you fancy going the whole forty days, like Jesus did in the wilderness, then I wouldn't suggest that you do it any more than once every decade! If you're planning on fasting for a week, maybe no more than four times a year. One day a week

---

[27] http://www.allaboutfasting.com/breaking-a-fast.html 25/09/2017 15:00

is splendid though as it's attainable and regular. My granddad used to do that. He wasn't a practising Christian, but he never had a problem with his weight and lived to a very old age, and I'm sure it had a lot to do with the fact he fasted each week. It still needed discipline and self-control but, as I've testified, had marvellous benefits.

7. EXERCISE

I couldn't find any instances in the bible where anyone really 'exercised' as people exercised as part of their daily lives, in those days. They had to walk to the market and synagogue, make bread, sweep the floor and fetch water. There weren't any cars, escalators, vacuum cleaners, dishwashers, washing machines or any of the appliances (that take all the exercise out of life) that we have today. And the appliances we have are becoming easier to use! Faster, remote controlled, touch screen and so they're having an ever-increasing impact on our lives –

and not a good one! Unfortunately, this coupled with the fact that food is constantly available means that we're not processing the calories we're eating, as fast as we should.

> People in biblical times had to exercise, we have the choice to exercise or not.

We do have more fun ways to exercise now though, but whereas they **had** to do them, now we have a **choice**.

What I did find in the bible, that has a small connection regarding exercise, is this:

Ephesians 6:15 And with your feet fitted with the **readiness** that comes from the gospel of peace.

Now, if you know your bible, you'll know this is in relation to the armour of God, as I said, it is a small connection. So, why have I used it? Well first, because it means that we need to be fit enough for the calling the Lord has placed and could place on

> We need to be fit for the calling that has been placed on our lives.

our lives. It's all very well in our comfy, central heated homes not to be fit, but what would happen if we were called to go to remote places in Africa or Asia where the main mode of transport was our very own legs! But as a lot of us aren't called to the "exotic" mission field (as it were) that may not seem to have much relevance. However, we are all called to serve, to show those around us that we love them, that we're willing to go the extra mile for them (Matthew 5:41). So, for this too we need to be in tip top condition.

Benefits of exercise

There are so many, countless benefits that we can reap from exercising regularly. Our first motive is that it burns calories and builds up muscle.[28] There are also all of these bonuses as it helps build; strength, stamina, co-ordination, balance, flexibility, the ability to sleep, breathing and enjoyment. If you thought that wasn't enough, it reduces the risk of major illnesses such as heart disease, stroke, osteoporosis, type 2 diabetes, bowel and breast cancer and early death. It boosts self-esteem, mood, sleep quality and energy. It also reduces stress, depression and dementia.[29] Wow!

Heart disease, circulation and strokes: When you exercise, the heart works more, the blood is pushed through the arteries faster, so it clears debris along the way. This then makes the

---

[28] https://www.healthline.com/health/diet-and-weight-loss-fitness-exercise 25/09/2017 15:29

[29] http://www.nhs.uk/Livewell/fitness/Pages/whybeactive.aspx 25/09/2017 15:31

whole system work with more efficiency, which prevents blood clots, that can lead to heart attacks and strokes.[30] When you then rest, the heart also "rests" and decreases its rate so that it won't become overworked – this means that your heart will be able to cope better when you need to exercise, and relax easier when it's time to stop.

Breast and bowel cancer: Physical activity lowers the level of oestrogen in women, which is thought to help develop breast cancer. Exercise also helps the food we eat to move through our bowels. When food moves quickly, it reduces the amount of time it's inside the bowel and so there's less chance of the food causing damage, which could lead to bowel cancer.[31]

Osteoporosis: When we get to a certain age, our bodies think, "Well I've had my kids, I'm not doing as much as I used to, I'm just sitting down all day. There's not much point in making new tissues as I'm not using them." Which then causes osteoporosis. However, when we exercise, the messages being sent to our bodies change and instead they think, "I need to be ready, I need to maintain my density and power because they're using me all the time. It must be a necessity." Hence, when we exercise the signals from our brains tell our tissues, bones and muscles they are needed, and to stay in tip top shape, so they don't deteriorate.[32]

---

[30] http://www.netdoctor.co.uk/healthy-living/a1168/exercise-heart-disease-and-high-blood-pressure/ 25/09/2017 15:40

[31] http://www.cancerresearchuk.org/about-cancer/causes-of-cancer/physical-activity-and-cancer/how-physical-activity-prevents-cancer 25/09/2017 16:41

[32] http://www.webmd.com/osteoporosis/features/exercise-for-osteoporosis#1 28/09/2017 14:11

Diabetes: When we eat something a chemical reaction happens inside our bodies and glucose is created, this glucose is used up straight away when we exercise and so is fine. However, if we don't exercise, the pancreas creates insulin to turn the glucose into fat and store it away. If this continues for a long period of time, not only do the fat stores build up to critical levels but the stress being caused to our pancreases finally makes them pack up and stop working. Then, the levels of glucose in our blood becomes critical and we need injections of insulin to combat it – this is diabetes. Exercise then reduces the risk of diabetes and the need for insulin as it consumes the glucose quickly, preventing it from going into the blood.[33]

Depression: A few years ago, I was probably clinically depressed. I went to the doctors a couple of times talking about my low state of mind, but really didn't want to go on any tablets so the appointments didn't help. What helped were the exercise classes I was doing. I could start a class feeling tired, low and depressed, but after, I always felt

> I could start an exercise class feeling tired and low, and end up having the best one ever!

great. It worked every time! I could have an argument with my husband before a class and after, forget all the hurt and contention. It doesn't make sense but the worse I felt, the better the class! For a start, I think it just took my mind off my problems and I concentrated on something trivial, then all the negative energy I had, was poured out into the physical activity and I was able to relax. Jesus really helped me at that time, too,

---

[33] http://www.diabetes.co.uk/exercise-for-diabetics.html 28/09/2017 14:18

but I was grateful I was able to exercise as well. Now, since the depression has left, I still love the exercise and it still makes me feel great.

Losing weight: Now of course, we're also interested in exercise as a way of losing and controlling our weight and the great news is, if you enjoy exercise and do it enough you may not need to diet at all!! That would be ideal, wouldn't it? Did you know that muscle weighs more than fat though? – So, don't be put off, if the scales seem to contradict your new lifestyle and inch loss. Another great thing is, muscle burns more calories even when

Even when we're resting, muscles burn off more calories than fat.

resting than fat does,[34] so even when we aren't doing anything, if we've changed our body masses to be mainly muscle, we'll still be burning more calories. It also looks a lot more flattering, as muscle doesn't bounce or wobble as much as fat!

What to do?

There are so many different forms of exercise around, we can really take our pick. Even just round the house, we can make changes to our routines, to make more exercise for ourselves; we could sweep the floors instead of vacuuming them – if they're laminated anyway, wash up – rather than using dishwashers, run up the stairs rather than walking. Then, outside the house, gardening is cheap, and what a reward it is, if we have an exterior full of colour afterwards! Wash the car – don't take it to the

---

[34] https://www.healthline.com/health/diet-and-weight-loss-fitness-exercise#benefits4 28/09/2017 14:59

garage over the road!! (By the way these ideas will save electricity and keep you warm, saving money on those utility bills too!) Always be the first to do something. If someone wants a drink - jump up to make it! Don't procrastinate, don't put it off, don't say, "Well he who has the vision gets the mission!" Let's be people who are always ready to serve, always the first ones up to do a task, a chore, a run!

Fidgeting is great (some people do it as a by-product from worry, others just do it because it's a habit) – I've looked at websites that give figures about how many calories we can lose just by fidgeting and they're amazing – however I think it's more of an individual thing, rather than generic. The point though, is that it's burning calories. Whenever we're doing something, glucose is being used to carry out the task, rather than sitting in fatty deposits around our bodies. So, don't sit still for longer than fifteen minutes at a time. If we're watching a film, we should get up and make a drink, go to the toilet, run on the spot for a couple of minutes, or do something, during the adverts! When we're sitting at our desks, we can lift the bottom half of our legs or do some stretches every now and then. Even pulling in our stomach muscles will help – surely! I think most of us have been on a plane one time or another, well, when the deep vein thrombosis thing was big news, the planes used to show some exercises we could do in our seats, just to get our blood circulating. Guess what? We can do those anywhere now! Whether we're in an office, at the cinema or on a bus!!! Just circle our heads, go onto the balls of our feet, circle our shoulders

> **Don't sit still for longer than fifteen minutes at a time.**

and lift our arms. As I keep saying – "JUST DO SOMETHING!"

I'm a great believer in walking and I'm sure this is one thing we can all do. I love my family and friends but one thing that exasperates me about some of them, is they'll use their car to just pop to the shops, which are approximately 200 yards away, and then complain they're putting on weight! We should leave the car on the drive, and walk! It'll probably be quicker, save congestion, better for the environment and better for us! When we walk, we shouldn't just stroll along at a slow saunter either, but go a bit faster! Go, so that we feel our hearts beating at a quicker rate, if we start breathing heavily, don't worry, it just means we're doing it properly because we're taking more oxygen in, to burn off the glucose, around our systems.

There are so many other things we can do too! Running, swimming, cycling, playing a sport, fitness classes, dancing, going to the gym; I'm sure all of us can find something that we enjoy, which I think is one of the main keys. If we like what we do, we're far more likely to keep it up. Whatever we choose, it doesn't have to take hours each day, even just ten minutes a day will have a dramatic effect on your life, although the experts are saying we need to do 150 minutes a week.[35] Which works out to be 25 minutes per day, over six days, I don't think that sounds too much, do you?

> **Just ten minutes every day will have a dramatic effect on your life.**

---

[35] http://www.nhs.uk/Livewell/fitness/Pages/physical-activity-guidelines-for-adults.aspx 28/09/2017 15:21

The hardest thing though, is endurance – to keep it up.

Hebrews 10:36 For you have need of steadfast patience and **endurance**, so that you may perform and fully accomplish the will of God, and thus receive and carry away (and enjoy to the full) what is promised. (AMP)

But if we can keep it up, just look at those rewards – we'll receive and carry away what is promised!

I know that, if I were to join a gym, I would go for a few weeks and then stop. It would be a waste of time and money and I would feel guilty and bad about it afterwards. So, as I was dancer in my past, and am reliable when other people are depending on me, I opened a dance school. Since then I've started teaching Zumba and other fitness classes. They're great! I'm exercising five hours a week and getting paid for it! I have also done kick boxing classes, and really enjoyed those too, as it was a great way of meeting people and having a good laugh (both of which we discussed in another chapter!) If you don't know what you want to do yet, maybe a good plan would be to do different forms of exercise each month: such as running January, cycling February, squash March and so on, then you wouldn't get bored. (Or, if those sound way to energetic for now, why not do: swimming January, table tennis February and salsa classes March?) When we begin a new activity, there's always a lot of motivation, as it's exciting and new. This way it

> When we begin something new there's a lot of motivation, so start something new each month!

105

would be starting something new every month – and still exercising and keeping fit!

A warning though, when I used to stop regular exercise, in my younger years, (such as going home from boarding school for holidays, and in between dancing contracts – so it would be for a couple of weeks, at least) I would have feelings of depression, I had problems keeping my temper and my muscles would feel awful, so please keep going!

Rest

Resting rather than stopping is really important though, so I would recommend taking time to do this, a few minutes every day and one day a week. Not resting sleeping, not resting watching the television, but really resting. The Lord Himself rested on the seventh day to show us how important it is, world class athletes rest and it's important for us to do it too.

Psalm 46:10 Be **still**, and know that I am God.

> Jesus wants us to know Him intimately.

At times, it's important to do nothing and simply meditate on the Lord. But why? It's because He wants **us to know Him** intimately. He loves us so much He wants to spend all His time with us! He loves us so much He is completely interested in us, all the time! And He wants us to know Him just as much! If we knew Him properly our lives would certainly change completely. There would be no need to worry, as we'd know our needs are met fully in Him, such as our needs to be loved and accepted.

Resting to know that **He is** God. Not just that He was God, but that He IS! That there is no end to Him, that He is with us, that He is Lord of all. That He is God, the Maker of heaven and earth. The Maker of planets that make our sun look tiny, the maker of

> Rest to know that He is God, not just that He was God, but that **He is!**

atoms so small we can't physically see them. The God Who made the sea part for the Israelites, the sea calm for the disciples and then Who walked on it as well! He is fully worthy of our time. Just stop and think about Him.

1 John 4:19 We love Him, because **He first** loved us. (KJV)

Wow, I've meditated on this scripture for a year and it still overwhelms me! The love of God is so incredible, I bathe in it, He loved me before I even knew of Him! Just think on that, be still and let His love wash over you, as you are, not as you will be, not as you were, but as you are. Then once we can get a grasp of His infinite love for us, it's easy to love Him back, it's easy to love others too, because it doesn't matter what they think of us. We can be secure in His love, even if our spouses leave us (like mine did) even if our friends desert us (like mine did). It doesn't matter, because the Lord is our source of love and acceptance – not man or people. We can love without fear, without being vulnerable, because we have the love that exceeds all understanding within us, from the highest power in heaven and earth.

Matthew 11:28-29 Come to Me, all you who are weary and burdened, and I will **give you rest**. Take my yoke upon you, and learn from me, for I am gentle and humble in heart, and you will find rest for your souls.

Isaiah 40:31 But **they that wait** upon the Lord shall renew their strength, they shall mount up with wings as eagles, they shall run, and not be weary; and they shall walk and not faint. (KJV)

Waiting always sounded negative to me. It conjured up waiting at checkouts, waiting for appointments or the bus. Lots of wasted time just hanging around, when I could've been doing something else. But here in Isaiah, it's a benefit. Waiting on the Lord, is not wasted time at all, as it builds our strength, helps us soar like eagles, walk and run! Sounds like the more we rest in the Lord and wait on Him, the more energy we'll get as a result! Isn't He truly, truly, truly wonderful! So, the next time we find ourselves waiting in a queue, maybe we should think on this verse and turn that wasted time into something productive.

> The more we wait on Him, the more energy we'll get as a result!

Going Forward

Make a plan to exercise, just like fasting, be determined in your thinking. Start by looking for ways you can do more around the house, garden and at work. Then find ways of increasing your heart rate more often.

What did you like doing as a child? What clubs are going on in your area? What have you always wanted to try? Take a look around, go on the Internet, ask the Lord to give you opportunities, maybe even start a club of your own. Don't be afraid or embarrassed, everyone has been a beginner at some point. When I began kick boxing, I didn't look pretty, I didn't have a clue what any of the exercises were, but it didn't last. I always remembered that I had paid for them too, which put me in control. If there was something I didn't like, I didn't do it. If there was something I didn't think I could do, I'd have a go, sometimes it worked, sometimes it didn't, but I tried. I encourage you to have a go too.

Lastly, look to build up the time you're exercising to 150 minutes a week and then don't forget to have some rest as well.

8. TEMPTATIONS

We're all tempted at times, but why and who is it that tempts us? Hopefully we don't believe that it's God who's trying to teach us something? I have a simple

God is good, the devil is bad.

philosophy: God is good and the devil is bad. Whenever anything good happens to me, I thank the Lord and whenever anything bad occurs, I blame the devil.

John 10:10 The thief (devil) comes only to steal and kill and destroy. I (Jesus) have come that they may have life, and have it to the full. (Brackets mine)

James 1:17 Every **good and perfect gift is from above**, coming down from the Father of the heavenly lights, who does not change like shifting shadows.

These verses clearly tell us God is good. Temptations can lead to bad things, so then temptations cannot come from Him:

James 1:13-15 When tempted, no-one should say, "God is tempting me." For God cannot be tempted by evil, **nor does He tempt anyone;** but each one is tempted when, by his own evil desire, he is dragged away and enticed. Then, after desire has conceived, it gives birth to sin; and sin, when it is full-grown, gives birth to death.

Here we have confirmation that God is **not** the cause of our temptations at all. They're from our own thoughts and desires. I don't smoke and have never liked it the few times I've tried.

You could wave a thousand cigarettes at me, blow smoke in my face, make loving noises whilst you puffed away and it wouldn't do a thing for me. No matter what you do I would not be tempted to have a drag! But wave a cream cake at me, or just have it on a table where I can see it and it's a different story! Why? Because I enjoy them, I have experienced them. I remember what they taste like and so based on those good memories: I want them. Notice, neither of these instances have involved God at all. No, when we're tempted it's because of our own desires which the devil uses against us.

> The devil used food to tempt man in the Garden of Eden and Jesus in the wilderness.

The devil's first ever temptation to man involved food and his first recorded temptation to Jesus involved food too. So, it's logical to think that the devil would also use food to tempt us. That could put us off eating right away – let the devil win? Oh no thank you!

But, let's look at what happened on the two occasions:

Adam and Eve

Genesis 3:1-6 Now the serpent was more crafty than any of the wild animals the Lord God had made. He said to the woman, "Did God really say, 'You must not eat from any tree in the garden'?" The woman said to the serpent, "We may eat fruit from the trees in the garden, but God did say, 'You must not eat fruit from the tree that is in the middle of the garden, and you must not touch it, or you will die.'"

111

"You will not surely die," the serpent said to the woman. "For God knows that when you eat of it your eyes will be opened, and you will be like God, knowing good and evil." When the woman saw that the fruit of the tree was good for food and pleasing to the eye, and also desirable for gaining wisdom, she took some and ate it. She also gave some to her husband, who was with her, and he ate it.

Adam and Eve had food in plentiful supply, like we have today. They could've gone out at any time of the day and night and had something to eat. They weren't hungry. They had everything they needed. There were trees everywhere, acres and acres of trees. Imagine yourself in a wood and how big it feels, well the garden of Eden was bigger than that! And the Lord simply told them not to eat from **one** of them. Could you pick out a single tree from a forest full of them? Adam and Eve probably didn't even notice the tree was there, until the devil pointed it out. He simply tempted them with the one and only thing they weren't allowed. Eve focused on what she didn't have, instead of what she did. Are we the same? Are we just miserable because we can't have **one** thing?

> There were trees everywhere, acres and acres of them, the Lord simply told them not to eat from **one** of them.

The Lord knew it would be bad for them if they ate the fruit. He wasn't withholding anything good from them, instead He just wanted to spare them from pain and death. But the devil turned it around and made Adam and Eve believe they were missing out on something good. Do we think we're missing out on something good when we know we shouldn't have it? Like fizzy drinks for instance? Or (in reality) are we just missing out on a load of bad stuff! Are we tempted into thinking, it must be great just because we're not allowed it? Because it's a lie. An added thought – the commentary never actually said the fruit tasted nice! Isn't it the same with us? We know we shouldn't eat

> **The Lord does not withhold anything that is good for us!**

something and then when we do, it doesn't even taste that great! We need to remember the Lord's goodness – **He is not going to withhold anything that is good for us** and only turn us away from things that are bad.

Another reason Eve didn't resist the temptation, was because she looked at the fruit. How many times could we avoid temptations if we simply didn't look! It's such an easy thing to do – really. Many times, we say "I might be on a diet, but I can still look at the menu!" but doesn't Jesus say that if your eye causes you to sin – pluck it out? Now I'm not saying pluck your eyes out, to avoid looking – JUST DON'T LOOK!!!! Then after she looked, she desired it. Our senses will promote desire. Smells, appearance, sounds, they all make us want things. If you find yourself desiring food – walk away, go somewhere else, give your senses something else to think about.

And then, Eve gave in and took the fruit. What a shame! Here it is again:

Genesis 3:6 When the woman **saw** that the fruit of the tree was GOOD for food and pleasing to the eye, and also desirable for gaining WISDOM, she took some and ate it.

Notice how the words in capital letters are words that are normally used to describe God. Good and wise. It also said at the beginning of the passage that the devil used a crafty beast, and he used a subtle strategy because, as we can see, he tempted them with something that looked like it would benefit them. He has the same strategy with us, making us think it will make us feel better. That it'll fill the void. But the truth is, it won't!!! I think that we all know that, in our heart of hearts, we know it's wrong, but our flesh is so strong that it tends to dominate us too often.

Jesus

So now let's have a look to see how Jesus handled his temptation:

Matthew 4:1-4 Then Jesus was led by the Spirit into the desert to be tempted by the devil. After fasting for forty days and forty nights, He was hungry. The tempter came to Him and said, "If you are the Son of God, tell these stones to become bread." Jesus answered, **"It is written**: 'Man does not live on bread alone, but on every Word that comes from the mouth of God."

The setting for Jesus' temptation starts off completely opposite to Adam and Eve's situation – and our own – as He hadn't eaten for forty days. He's also in the desert, as opposed to a plentiful garden, so there isn't abundant food everywhere. Satan tempts Him where He's at His most vulnerable.

> Jesus used the Word of God to resist temptation.

114

So, here's the most important bit – the way Jesus resisted it – He used the Word of God, scripture that He had memorised and meditated on and this is where He found it.

Deuteronomy 8:3 To teach you that man does not live on bread alone but on every Word, that comes from the mouth of the Lord.

If Jesus used the Word against the devil, then we should too! But, we need to know the Word, to be able to use it, so that when we're tempted, we can use it as a weapon against the devil and overcome him.

A long time ago, I asked the Lord what spiritual warfare was. And a few years later He answered me! It probably took that long to get an answer, due to my lack of knowledge in the Word (I am not accusing the Lord of tardiness at all!) And what was the answer? It was found in the story of David and Goliath! When David went out to fight Goliath, he chose five smooth stones. (1 Samuel 17:40) Why did he pick smooth stones? Surely if you were going to use a stone to kill someone (please bear in mind I'm not an Olympic sling shot or an assassin) you would use jagged stones, according to my logic, as they would have the most effect! But no, David chose smooth ones, and they worked!

Likewise, the Lord has provided us with weapons to use against the devil. They're not jagged; they're not loud, they're not angry or physical. They're smooth; they're tender, they're formed out of love, faith and

> Our spiritual weapons are formed out of love and faith.

good things. Who would think, rationally, that praise and prayer would have such a dramatic effect on the devil? But they do! He can't stand it when we praise the Lord, and he flees! God however, inhabits our praise and is attentive to our prayers. Love and grace are weapons too, the devil hasn't got anything to fight us with, when we act in love towards God, others and ourselves. And if we grasp the Lord's grace and the fact that He has overcome all the schemes of the devil on our behalf, he can't have any power over us.

> The devil can't stand it when we praise the Lord and flees!

The armour of God

We have been given armour too, Ephesians 6 is a well-known part of scripture, that lists the armour of God, we have at our disposal. The belt of truth is first; because we need to know the truth about the Lord's thoughts for us and His good will for us. We need to know that His way is the best way, that He doesn't want anything bad for us but only that which is good. The belt is at the centre of our bodies, the truth needs to be the centre of our thinking, and with it we will not be shamed or embarrassed.

The helmet of salvation, is worn on our heads. We need to know in our heads that we're saved. Saved from hell, saved from sickness, disease and yes, obesity. We are saved from all the schemes of hell and have been set aside for heaven, health and prosperity.

We also have the shield of faith and the sword of the Spirit, which is the Word of God, so that we can fight back as well and cause the devil to flee!

Who are we?

Note that Satan also tempted Jesus to doubt who He was. "If you are the Son of God," was what the devil said. Jesus needed to know who He really was to combat this subtle scheme, and so do we. Who are we? We are the children of God!

> Jesus needed to know who He was and so do we! We are the children of God!

Romans 8:15-16 For you did not receive a spirit that makes you a slave again to fear, but you received the **Spirit of sonship**. And by Him we cry, "Abba, Father." The Spirit Himself testifies with our spirit that we are **God's children**.

It gets even better than that!

Romans 8:17 Now if we are children, then we are **heirs** - heirs of God and co-heirs with Christ, if indeed we share in His sufferings in order that we may also share in His glory.

What about this one?

1John 4:17 Because in this world **we are like Him**. (Or the KJV says: As He is, so are we in this world.)

Are we getting to know who we are now? Are we beginning to see ourselves through God's eyes, and the devil's eyes? Now when Satan causes us to doubt who we are, these are the scriptures we need to remember and use against him.

Getting back to the subject

1 Corinthians 10:13 No temptation has seized you except what is common to man. And God is faithful; He will not let you be tempted beyond what you can bear. But when you are tempted, He will also provide **a way out** so you can stand up under it.

Isn't He great! God is with us in temptation and Jesus has provided a way for us to avoid it, all we have to do is remember and look for the escape route!

> Jesus is with us when we're tempted and provides an escape route!

He can also empathise with us and help us:

Hebrews 4:15-16 For we do not have a high priest who is unable to sympathise with our weaknesses, but we have One Who has been tempted in every way, just as we are – yet was without sin. Let us then approach the throne of grace with confidence, so that we may receive mercy and find grace to help us in our time of need.

Here's some of the ways we're able to withstand temptation:

- We have the Word of God written down, making it easier to remember correctly.
- We can learn by Adam and Eve's mistakes instead of making our own.

118

- Remember what we have, instead of what we don't.
- We don't have to be guided by our senses, feelings, emotions or situations, but we can trust in the authenticity and truth of the bible.
- We can bring captive every thought, every look, glance, want and desire.
- We can know what God wants for us. That He doesn't withhold anything good from us. That from the examples in the bible: God does know best.
- That we shouldn't be our own gods but that God is in control of us.
- Remember who we are.
- We have the Holy Spirit with us, all the time, and He will bring to remembrance the Word, so that we can fight and resist the devil.
- We have the fruits of the Spirit including self-control and patience.

We **are** on the winning side, the devil **is** defeated, and we **are** more than conquerors.

> We are on the winning side; the devil is defeated! We are conquerors.

Romans 8:37 No, in all these things we are **more than conquerors** through Him Who loved us.

1 John 4:4 You, dear children, are from God and have **overcome** them, because the One Who is in you is greater than the one who is in the world.

119

The Word changes us too!

The Word can also help us to change **our** minds as well – not only does it defeat the devil, but it can also have an impact on how **we** think. A long time ago, I was in a very tempting situation, I wanted to have a relationship with someone that wasn't suitable for me, he wasn't married, but he wasn't a Christian either and I knew we wouldn't have a future. But, I couldn't get him off my mind, even though I knew I should; I didn't know what to do! Thankfully the Lord was gracious to me and gave me scripture to help fight those thoughts:

Psalm 103:5 Who **satisfies** your desires with good things, so that your youth is renewed like the eagles.

Fantastic, my desires would be satisfied. Not granted but satisfied. That meant that the satisfaction must be equal to or exceeding the desire! As the desire was great, so must the satisfaction be! But not only would my desires be satisfied, they would be satisfied by good things, and nothing would harm me – as they would be satisfied by Him. I could look forward to good things coming my way. Not only that, my youth would be renewed like the eagles – I'm sure you would agree that's something worth having! I call it divine Botox! And, if He did that for me, He will do it for you too. He will satisfy your desires, whether it's for food or something else, He'll satisfy them with good things AND your youth will be renewed like the eagles!

> My desires would be satisfied, not granted but satisfied. As the desire was great so must the satisfaction!

James 1:12 **Blessed** is the man who perseveres under trial, because when he has stood the test, he will receive the crown of life that God has promised to those who love Him.

Both of these scriptures helped to completely transform my thinking back to His Word and promises, I was able to withstand the temptation until it finally left, and now when I look back on it, it's hard to believe it had such a grip on me. Thank you, God, with Your help I was able to conquer and overcome my desires. And with His help - you will too!

Going forward

First of all, try not to find yourselves in tempting situations, by not looking, instead think on what you can have, rather than what you can't.

Remember the truth. Is it good for you? Is it what you need? Does it even taste that great?

Finally, use the Word of God! Speak it out, meditate on His promises and turn away from those temptations, think on being satisfied in other ways and your youth being renewed instead.

9. GRACE – HIS UNMERITED FAVOUR

> Mercy = not getting what we deserve.
> Grace = getting what we don't deserve.

The words mercy and grace are used a lot in the bible, but what do they mean? We can't earn them and we can't make them. God has given them to us free of charge. Although they cost Him His Own Son. (That should tell us how much we're worth!) It's quite simple though really– mercy means **not** getting what we deserve, and grace means **getting** what we don't deserve! How amazing is that? We can get what we don't deserve!

The New Covenant

We all know the Ten Commandments/law, do not murder, do not bare false witness, etc. etc. but these are no longer in effect (it's beneficial to keep them, I certainly don't think it's a good idea to murder any one! And if you got caught you would go to jail – rightly so.) But, we won't experience the curses described in such places as Deuteronomy 28:15-68, if we do. God will still love us, keep His face turned towards us and bless us!

I bet you think I'm joking, don't you? But look at this next scripture, it talks about just this! We have a New Covenant, sealed with the blood of Jesus when He took all the wrath of God upon Himself and died on the cross for us. The Ten Commandments were in the Old Covenant, weren't they? Well, in the next verse, it says that the Old Covenant is obsolete. I looked up the word obsolete and some of its synonyms are: out of date, no longer in use, discarded, discontinued and extinct. This verse, found in the bible, is therefore saying the Old

Covenant (including the Ten Commandments) is out of date.[36] It's no longer in use, it's discarded, discontinued and extinct!

Hebrews 8:13 By calling this covenant "new," He has made the first one **obsolete**; and what is **obsolete** and ageing will soon disappear.

> When Jesus went to the cross He paid our price for every single curse.

When Jesus went to the cross and died He fulfilled the requirements of the law by being the blood sacrifice. He paid our price. One of the last things He said before he died was, "It is finished." What was finished? The curse. Every single curse. He became the curse for us, the curse that should've been on us if we broke the law. That is mercy - not getting what we deserve.

So now, we live in a completely different time than the Jews did under the law. We live under the New Covenant of grace. (getting what we don't deserve) Hallelujah!

But why did He have to remove the Old Covenant? Wasn't it good? Wasn't it God inspired? Well, yes of course it was, it prevented a lot of problems and showed humans how to live together and, most importantly, that we couldn't save ourselves but needed a saviour; as instead of getting rid of sin, the Ten Commandments/law highlighted it

> Instead of getting rid of sin, the law highlighted it and made it become appealing!

[36] https://en.oxforddictionaries.com/thesaurus/obsolete 02/10/2017 14:17

and made it become appealing! I know that sounds blasphemous, but I have biblical proof!

Rom 5:20 The law was added so that the trespass might **increase**.

1 Corinthians 15:56 ... the power of sin **is** the law.

Hebrews 7:19 For the law made **nothing** perfect ...

These scriptures are so radical! No wonder Jews were killing Christians! They went against everything they believed in! To think the law only made us sin more? But if you think about it, it makes sense. I'm sure when someone has told you not to do something – you want to do it more – like not eating cakes!

I went to a boarding school as a teenager. It was an all-girls school and we were there to learn dancing. Well as you can imagine, there were plenty of rules – there had to be, there were so many of us teenage girls running around! One of the rules, of course, was no smoking.

Well, as soon as I didn't get what I wanted or got told off for something I didn't feel was justified, I would smoke! Why? I've already told you I'm never tempted by cigarettes – they have no appeal to me. But I had one **because I knew I wasn't allowed to.** I wanted to smoke because I was told I couldn't. I was given a law and I was determined to break it.

> I wanted to smoke because I wasn't allowed to. I was given a law and I was determined to break it.

I see the same thing happening with my son. In fact, sometimes he hasn't even noticed the thing I'm telling him he's not allowed, but by pointing out something like a knife by saying, "Don't touch the knife" he realizes the knife is there and because there's a command not to do it, he wants to touch it! And let's face it when our spouses tell us to do something, we definitely dig our heels in then too!

So, instead of the law, God gave us the new covenant of grace, and the endings to the verses I've used before, show us this:

Romans 5:20 But where sin increased, **grace increased** all the more.

1 Corinthians 15:57 But thanks be to God! He gives us the **victory** through our Lord Jesus Christ.

Hebrews 7:19 ... a **better hope** is introduced, by which we draw near to God.

Thank You Jesus for grace! Thank You Jesus that I don't have to rely on following the rules, but following You. It takes away all my stress and worry, it takes away my restrictions and I feel free. Free to not sin. Free to do what I want, because I want to and not because there's a law saying I have to. And what I want, is to live in peace, to live in security, to live with You in my life Jesus. To not smoke, to not overeat, to live Your way. Amen.

> Thank you, Jesus, that I'm free. Free to do what I want. Free to not sin.

Masters of sin

Romans 6:14 For **sin shall not be your master**, because you are not under the law, but under grace.

So, if the Ten Commandments aren't in force anymore, why does the New Testament still talk about sin? What is it? We can find out in John 16, where it says that the Holy Spirit will convict the world of sin, and follows on to explain what it is:

John 16:9 In regard to **sin**, because men do not **believe** in Me.

The only sin we can still commit with consequences is not believing in Jesus. When we look to other things to bring the benefits that Jesus can (and wants) to give us, we are not **believing** in His provision and so sinning. So then, when we look to overeating to provide comfort and relief, instead of going to Jesus, we could call this sin too. We trust in the power of food more than we believe in the power of God. But just look at the verse from Romans again. If we're born-again believers who are filled with the Spirit, **sin will not be our masters**. It isn't lord in our lives any more.

> When we look to other things rather than believing Jesus, we sin.

So why are we still sinning then? Because our minds haven't been renewed. Because as we think we have no control over sin, we don't. Once we realise that we're in control and that we have the resources to fight it, we will and we'll win!

As I've already stated overeating can be classed as a sin, so then we can change the word "sin," in the scripture, to one that fits our circumstances such as, "food," and then we can say: "Food will not be our masters;" or stomachs, "Our stomachs will not be our masters." Wow that's good isn't it! Food can't entrap us any longer because we don't belong to the world's systems any more, instead we belong to Christ. We are under grace.

Grace not works

Ephesians 2:8-9 For it is by **grace** you have been saved, through faith – and this not from yourselves, it is the gift of God – **not by works**, so that no-one can boast.

If we have given our lives to Jesus, no matter what we do, the Lord will love us and has saved us from an eternity in hell. And that's wonderful! But He didn't just save us from hell; He also saved us from sickness, addiction, bondage and poverty. He has saved us from the addiction to food; all we have to do is accept it. He wants to favour us! He wants to give us gifts!

> He has saved us from the addiction to food, all we have to do is accept it.

What better favour and gifts could we have than being slim, fit and healthy? The Lord wants these for us and has provided these things for us. Again, all we have to do is accept them! However, if we seek to be slim through the law – counting calories, fat content and carbohydrate content, which start off being quite fun and make a quick difference, we may find ourselves in bondage and under a heavy burden. As we've taken Christ out of the situation.

Galatians 5:4 You who are trying to be **justified by law** have been alienated from Christ: you have fallen **away from grace**.

From that verse we see that if we only follow rules and laws we fall from grace! To avoid that, we need to believe in His goodness, provision and ability rather than our own. That He has completed the work of redemption and taken away all our weaknesses and sorrows when He died on the cross. He has paid the price for us to be healthy. He has paid the price for all our sins from the past, the sins we do today and the ones we haven't yet committed. He's paid for all the sins we know about and the ones we don't. We are free! We are saved!

Freedom!

Everyone should now be asking, "Can we just carry on overeating then, if that's the case?" But as Paul answered the question, "Shall we go on sinning?" in Romans 6:1, "God forbid!" I will also say, "No way!" "Not on your Nelly!" Why? Paul gives us two reasons; the first, because we've died to our old nature. When we gave our lives to the Lord and were born again, we became new creatures. The old creatures that were ruled by our bodies, lusting for food, drink and all the rotten stuff, died. We left our old ways with our old natures that were buried with Him when He was crucified, and instead we have new natures that are in Christ.

> "Can we just carry on eating whatever we want then?" "No way!"

Romans 6:1-4 What shall we say, then?   Shall we go on sinning, so that grace may increase? (God forbid KJV) By no means! We **died** to sin; how can we live in it any longer? Or don't you know that all of us who were baptised into Christ Jesus were baptised into His death? We were therefore **buried** with Him through baptism into death in order that, just as Christ was raised from the dead through the glory of the Father, we too may live a new life.

2 Corinthians 5:17 Therefore, if anyone is in Chris, he is a **new creation**; the old has gone, the new has come!

Does a dead person want cakes or crave chocolate?	Can a dead person want cakes? Can a dead person crave chocolate? No! We have died to sin, our wants and cravings, we left them in the grave and now we live for Christ, in newness of life without our weaknesses, which held us back.

Romans 6:7 because anyone who has **died** has been **freed** from sin.

The second reason, is that when we give into something, it becomes our masters. I've already mentioned this before but it needs saying again as it's probably where the main problem is. By giving into it, the sin or food (or whatever it is) can get a hold of us and make us its slaves!

Romans 6:15-16 What then? Shall we sin because we are not under law but under grace? By no means! Don't you know that when you offer yourselves to someone to obey him as **slaves**, you are slaves to the one whom you obey – whether you are **slaves** to sin, which leads to death, or to obedience, which leads to righteousness?

Let's not be slaves to sin or food, let's be slaves to Christ. Thank Jesus that He has redeemed us from our bondages; all we have to do is change our minds to obey the Word and follow Christ.

1 Corinthians 6:12 "Everything is permissible for me" – but not everything is beneficial.

So, here's the crux of the matter: it's not whether we can sin and get away with it! But whether it's going to be good for us? Will it benefit us? These are the questions we always need to consider. And of course, the answer will always be, "No." Sin is never the answer, it will never help us. Jesus is our answer, He will help us. Christ made us free of sin when we became born again, so why would we want to become entrapped by it again?

> Sin is never the answer, it will never help us.

Like a tightrope

The Lord gave me a picture of a tightrope walker. The tightrope was grace and the falls to either side being the two ways we can fall from it. If we go one side towards legalism, we think that just by doing things correctly we'll earn the favour of God. However, that would be making ourselves self-righteous – there would've been no need for Jesus to die, in that case. If we go to the other side, towards liberalism, and just do what we want or

130

desire without thought or concern for what is right, going contrary to the Word of God, then we can become ensnared in sin and entrapped. It could bind us up, so that we forget we're slaves to righteousness and a temple of the Holy Spirit. Thankfully the safety net of God's abundant grace always catches us and put us back on the tightrope. And as we practise more and more, it becomes easier.

Sin takes work!

One of my favourite verses is:

Romans 6:23 For the wages of sin is death, but the gift of God is eternal life in Jesus Christ our Lord.

We get wages, once we've worked! Implying that it takes work to sin! Whilst the "gift of God is eternal life." It doesn't take any work to get a gift; in fact, all we have to do is to receive it! We get the gift anyway, let's not squander it by working to sin.

Galatians 5 lists the "Fruits of righteousness."

Galatians 5:22-23 But the fruit of the Spirit is love, joy, peace, patience, kindness, goodness, faithfulness, gentleness and self-control. Against such things there is no law.

Natural fruit normally grows on trees. It doesn't have to try to grow, it doesn't labour to grow – it does so naturally! Likewise, spiritual fruits such as self-control and patience will grow naturally in our lives if we just let them! Fantastic!

Unfortunately, we want to do it in our own strength, don't we? Our egos actually imagine we can overcome sin/food ourselves! We want to do it our way, and we want to do it now! We don't want to wait and we want to do it so that it won't hurt our stomachs.

But we need to learn to put ourselves out of the picture. It's a very humbling experience, really waiting on the Lord, realising He has done all the work for us. He has paid the price and, He has suffered the punishment. Nothing we do now will add to that cost or diminish it. All we can do is choose what to follow. To follow our bodies which are not in the process of becoming renewed or follow the Spirit which is prompting us to move towards life, love and freedom. We were never made to overcome sin ourselves, but to accept that Jesus has already overcome it for us and go forward in liberty. We can't do it in our own strength; we've tried and probably failed. He's God. Not us, so let's do it His way!

> **Nothing** we do will add to the price Jesus paid for us on the cross.

Going forward

Let go of food, the worry of eating too much, the comfort we believe it provides and instead rely on Jesus who never fails. He has the power to heal and deliver us from food. He will fulfil our needs: spiritually, mentally and physically. Fill up on the Lord, let Him be our portions, by thinking, speaking and using the Word of God.

As you go on, I pray that the ideas in this book, come to your mind and have a positive impact on your life. I pray that you get to know the Lord more and more, and He becomes ever increasingly important to you. I also pray that the weight you want to lose, goes and doesn't return and that instead you gain freedom and success in its place.

Amen.

ACKNOWLEDGEMENTS

This book has taken a long time to write! I started a Slim with Him group at my local church over ten years ago and I was persuaded then to put the tips into a book. There have been many drafts since then and reasons why it has taken me so long to finish, but thankfully now it's complete!

Anyway, through the process I've had a lot of help from my friends and family, and I would like to thank them here. Many took the time to read through the scripts and give their honest opinions and many others helped me to design and photograph the front cover – which took a lot longer than anticipated!

I would also like to thank the amazing pastors that have supported me over the years, and the teaching I've received that has transformed my thinking from religion to grace. From thinking I had to act, speak and think in a certain way, to fully relying on Jesus and His sacrifice instead. That He has saved me and nothing that I do now, either right or wrong, can change that. My only responsibility is to believe in Him, to believe that He loves me and that He wants what is best for me.

Mostly, I would like to thank Jesus Himself, for always being there every step (or rather word) of the way. Thank You for making me stubborn and never giving up on it. Thank You for Your inspiration and amazing grace. Thank you, Lord. Amen.